Illuminate Publishing

WJEC

GCSE

Media Studies

Study and Revision Guide

Christine Bell

Published in 2014 by Illuminate Publishing Ltd, P.O. Box 1160,
Cheltenham, Gloucestershire GL50 9RW

Orders: Please visit www.illuminatepublishing.com
or email sales@illuminatepublishing.com

British Library Cataloguing in Publication Data

A catalogue record for this book is available from the British Library

ISBN 978-1-908682-21-5

Printed by CPI Group (UK) Ltd, Croydon, CR0 4YY
03.16

The publisher's policy is to use papers that are natural, renewable and recyclable
products made from wood grown in sustainable forests. The logging and
manufacturing processes are expected to conform to the environmental regulations
of the country of origin.

Copyright note:

Editor: Geoff Tuttle

Design and layout: Nigel Harriss

Acknowledgements

The author and publisher wish to thank the following students for allowing us to
showcase their work,

Phoebe Casey Miller
Sarah Donnelly
Hazem Jouda
Tiana Kirkwood
Yasamin Panahi
Joe Payne
Rachel Priestley
Clare Shepherd
William Smith

Jo Johnson for her invaluable support, advice and encouragement from concept
through to publication

Contents

Introduction 5

How to use this book 6

Section I: What is the Media? 8

Media texts 8
Media habits 10
Audiences 11
Media issues 11
Media organisations 13

Section 2: Introduction to the Media Studies Framework 15

Exploring genre 16
Exploring narrative 19
Exploring representation 20
Audience 22

Section 3: A Toolkit for Analysis 27

Signs and codes
Visual codes 28
Analysing audio-visual media texts 29
Audio codes 33
Analysing print texts 33
Analysing media texts: putting it all together 36

Section 4: What is a Topic? 37

The examination: Section A – Investigating 38
The examination: Section B – Planning 39
Controlled Assessment 40

Section 5: Television Crime Drama: Unit I Case Study 41

Formats and sub-genres 42
Media organisations 44
Media texts: analysing crime dramas 48
Narrative 51
Representation 53
Audience 55
Textual investigation: narrative 57

Section 6: Advertising and Marketing 59

Introduction 60
Techniques used by advertisers 61
Internet advertising 64
Audiences 64
Analysing a print advertisement 66
Analysing an advertising campaign: IRN-BRU 67
Section B practice assignment 70
Textual investigation: representation 71

Section 7: Lifestyle and Celebrity 73

Celebrities and media organisations 74
Text: representation of celebrities in the media 75
Audience: Dyer's Star theory 77
Practical assignment 80
Textual investigation: the representation of an issue 81

Section 8: The Vampire/Horror Genre 83

Introduction to vampires 83
Text: analysing film posters 85
Text: analysing film trailers 88
Text and organisations: investigating film and TV extracts 89
Practical assignment 92
Textual investigation: genre 93

Section 9: Music 95

Introductory activities 95
Text: music magazines 95
The magazine industry 99
Practice production assignment 99
Text: narrative – analysing a music video 100
Text: analysing CD covers 102
Text: analysing music websites 103
Textual investigation: narrative 104

Section 10: Controlled Assessment – Approaching Production 106

Research 106
Planning 110
Production 112
Evaluation 116
Production Planning Sheet 118
Storyboard 119

Section 11: Approaching Textual Investigations 120

Textual investigation titles 120
Tips for completing Textual investigations 121
Success criteria 122
Sample responses 123

Section 12: Exam Practice and Technique 127

Section A 127
Section B 129
Dos and don'ts 130
Questions and answers 131
Planning sheet 139

Quickfire answers 140

Glossary 144

Index 149

Introduction

The aim of this GCSE is to:

- Teach you the skills to enable you to investigate different media texts.
- Develop your understanding of the media and the role it plays in your daily life.
- Develop your practical skills.

What sort of things will you do in this subject?

- **Think about the media** – understand how media texts are constructed and how to analyse them.
- Learn to use media vocabulary to help you to explore texts.
- Gain practical skills which may include: digital filming and editing; still photography and design and layout using programs like Photoshop.
- **Create for the media** – plan, produce and present your own media texts, for example magazine pages, short films, animated films, and advertisements.

How will I be assessed?

This GCSE course is 60% coursework and 40% examination.

You will produce an assessment file which will be made up of three pieces of work completed during the course and showing a range of skills.

In the examination you will be asked to respond to audio-visual or print-based resources from a set topic area and to complete some planning and creative tasks.

Section 4 of this study guide will give you more information on the exam and the Controlled Assessment.

What can I do to help myself?

- Broaden your experience of the media. For example, watch television programmes you don't normally watch, read a different magazine.
- Talk to other people about the media so that you can find out about what other people watch and listen to.
- Keep up to date about what is happening in the media, for example successful films and television programmes.
- Make sure that you meet the deadlines set by your teachers.

Key Term

The media
Is a form of mass communication that can give out messages, inform and entertain a large audience.

Tip

Learning about how film posters, magazine covers and other media texts are constructed will help you to produce your own texts effectively.

Tip

Understanding the course you are doing and what is expected of you will help you to achieve success.

How to use this book

The contents of this study and revision guide are designed to help you to achieve success in WJEC GCSE Media Studies. This book has been written specifically for the WJEC GCSE course you are taking and includes useful information to help you to perform well in the examination and the internally assessed unit.

There are sections for the following elements of the GCSE Media Studies specification:

Unit 1: Thinking about the Media: Investigating and Planning

Unit 2: Creating for the Media: Investigating and Producing

The first sections of the book aim to cover the knowledge required to explore and create media texts. They outline what makes a media text and a topic and introduce the Media Studies Framework. There is a 'Toolkit' to help you to investigate a range of media texts using analytical skills. There is also a section that helps you to prepare for the examination.

Further sections explore a range of topics including, Television Crime Drama, Advertising and Marketing, Lifestyle and Celebrity, the Vampire Horror Genre and Music.

Each of these sections includes:

- An introduction to the topic.
- Examples of how to investigate a range of media texts including relevant terminology.
- Definitions of key terms and how to use them to help you in your revision.
- Quickfire questions designed to test your knowledge and understanding of the topic.

Key Term

- Tips based on the experience of teaching GCSE Media Studies over a period of years and designed to help you to improve your internally assessed assignments and your examination technique.

- Tasks to encourage you to apply the knowledge and understanding outlined in this study guide to develop your understanding of the examples you have studied in class. These tasks will include ideas for Textual investigations as well as practice planning and production tasks.

- Key figures linked to the theories you need to know and independent research tasks to broaden your knowledge and make you aware of the broader issues linked to the topic.

It is important to remember that this is a guide and although there are examples of annotated texts to help you, it is more important that you gain the knowledge and understanding to allow you to analyse any media texts including your own independently researched examples. The idea is that you will also apply the knowledge and understanding gained from this book to develop your understanding of media texts you have studied in class with your teacher.

Tip

TASK

Key Figure

Internally assessed work

Another section of the book covers the key skills for success with your internally assessed work, which is worth 60% of your final grade. Here you will find information about how to approach the production unit including examples of work from 'real' students to help to guide you in the decisions you make and to illustrate sections of this unit. The guide to writing Textual investigations will also include extracts from students' work and tips on how to plan and structure this element of your internally assessed work.

Finally, at the end of the book you will find some supplementary material to help your learning. This includes a glossary of media terminology.

Most importantly, you should take responsibility for your own learning and not rely on your teachers to give you notes or tell you how to gain the grades that you require. You should look for additional notes to support your study into WJEC GCSE Media Studies.

You can look at the WJEC website www.wjec.co.uk. In particular, you need to be aware of the specification. Look for specimen examination papers and mark schemes. You may find past papers useful as well as, although the topics change, you will be able to see the structure of the different sections of the paper.

Tip

Referring to key figures in the media and relevant theories will help you to show your broader understanding of the subject.

I: What is the Media?

You have chosen to study this subject at GCSE and it is important that you understand what is meant by 'the media'. A general definition of the media is that it is a way of communicating that reaches a lot of people. It can give out messages, inform and entertain a large audience. Using this definition the media includes:

- Television
- Film
- Newspapers
- Magazines and comics
- Radio
- Music
- Websites
- Computer games
- Advertising.

Media texts

What is produced by the media is called a **media text**. For example, a television programme is a media text, as is a music video.

It is important to explore the media and its role in our lives in a bit more detail in order to develop a broader understanding.

Task

In pairs, discuss each of the following statements about the media. Do you think they are true, false or a bit of both? Try not to give 'yes' or 'no' answers but to give clear, detailed reasons for what you are saying. Support your opinion by specific examples.

- The media does not really affect people on a day to day basis.
- The media is mostly used for entertaining people.
- Some types of media are more popular than others.
- The media can be used to influence the way people think.
- What we see and hear in the media is always true.
- Politicians use the media.
- The media is not important to stars and celebrities.
- The media can be very persuasive.
- The aim of the media is to make money.

Quickfire 1

Why is it important to understand the media and what it does?

In your discussion of the statements on page 8 you will have realised that the media is very important and very powerful. It is all around us every day and often we are not even aware that it has an effect on us. We are all media audiences and as you start to study this subject it is important to consider how you use the media and your specific **media habits**. You can then compare these with other people and begin to see that we all use the media and are affected by it in different ways.

To start with, try to estimate your **media consumption**. Fill in the table below for an average week (monthly for going to the cinema).

Watching a TV programme: On a television On another device, name the device, for example, laptop	*everyday*
Reading a magazine: Online version Print version	
Reading a newspaper: Online version Print version	
Listening to the radio	
Listening to music	
Playing computer games Format e.g. Playstation	
Going to the cinema (monthly) **Watching films at home**	
Using the Internet/social media	

Feedback your answers to the rest of the class. Are there differences between the ways in which people of your age consume the media? Think about how someone older than you, for example your parents or an older relative, may fill in this table differently. What do you think would change and why?

Key Terms

Media habits
This refers to the media texts we use regularly, for example watching a soap opera at the same time every week or reading the same magazine each month.

Media consumption
This is how much of the media we are exposed to and use on a daily basis.

Quickfire 2

Why might people of different ages consume the media differently?

Media habits

Now think in a bit more detail about the media texts you consume regularly so that you can build up a picture of your media habits and how they may be different from those of other people.

What are your favourite media texts?

Television programme?

Magazine/comic?

Radio station or particular programme?

Film you have seen recently?

Advertisement?

Computer game?

Choose one of the texts above and explore why you like it in more detail. Mention:

- Briefly what your text is. It will help to explain the **genre** and other relevant details, for example when it is **scheduled** if it is a television programme.

- Why you like it. Give specific examples from the text to explore what it is about the text that appeals to you. If it is a film, for example, you may be attracted by the genre or the stars.

- The **target audience** and how the text tries to attract and appeal to them.

- How you would sum up your chosen text if you were trying to persuade someone else to watch/read/play or listen to it.

Now compare your answers with the rest of the class. You could also broaden the discussion to consider your least favourite media texts and why that is. Now you have a media profile of your class and their media habits.

Quickfire
3

Why do you think it is important to be aware of how much we are surrounded by the media?

My media day

Now you are going to think about how much you are exposed to the media from getting up in the morning to going to bed at night. This will give you some idea of how much the media is all around us and how much of a consumer of the media you are.

Keep a media diary

Task

Write a diary of your day exploring when and where you are exposed to different media texts. Don't forget to include things you may just see in passing, for example the advert for a new film you see on the side of a passing bus. Try to give as much detail as possible, don't just write, 'I listen to the radio in the morning', say which station, programme, presenter, etc.

Compare your day with other people in your class. What are the differences and similarities? Do people of your age group have similar media experiences?

Audiences

By considering which media texts you like and use, you are beginning to consider different audiences and their likes and dislikes. Studying and understanding audiences and their relationship with media texts is very important to this subject. Different audiences enjoy and respond to different media texts in different ways; for example, your granny's favourite comedy programme may be very different from the one you would choose.

Younger children may be more easily scared

Independent research: audience research

Try to find out more about the media habits of people who are a different age from you. You can do this in a number of ways:

● Interview someone older than you about their media habits. It may also be interesting to ask about their viewing/reading/listening habits when they were your age to make comparisons.

● Conduct a survey in your school to find out the media habits of different people. If your school has an intranet or a VLE, it may be helpful to use this.

● Set up a blog and encourage people to respond with their favourite programmes and why.

Media issues

The media generally and specific media texts are constantly being discussed and often criticised. You will read about television programmes in newspapers and magazines and hear about newspapers and advertisements on television programmes. There are many **issues** linked to the **media** at the moment that are under discussion, some have been around for a long time and some are new.

Tip

Carrying out different types of audience research throughout your media course will help you when it comes to this part of your GCSE Production assignment.

Tip

When you are doing audience research, for example interviewing someone, think carefully about the questions you ask so that you get the most information. Try not to ask questions which will give only a 'yes' or 'no' answer.

Quickfire
4

Why might older people respond differently to certain television programmes?

TASK

In small groups discuss the statements related to media issues below:

Celebrities and other important figures deserve their privacy from the media.

Consider:

- What is a private place?
- Film stars and footballers like the media attention when it suits them.
- Being in the media eye is part of being a celebrity.
- Everyone deserves some privacy.

Young people of both genders are exposed to unreal body images in the media today.

Consider:

- Images in magazines including men's magazines.
- Size zero models.
- Television programmes that have an obsession with body size.
- Possible impact.

Social networking sites have their advantages and disadvantages.

Consider:

- People actually talk to each other less and are losing the art of conversation.
- Advertisers can access audiences more easily.
- Possible harmful effects?

The amount of violence in films, television programmes and computer games means that audiences are becoming desensitised.

Consider:

- Changes in content over time.
- Possible effects on an audience.
- Specific examples.

Key Terms

Media issues
These are important areas of concern related to the media that are discussed among audiences and in other media texts.

Desensitised
This is where an audience is less shocked or upset by violence because they see so much of it in certain media texts.

Tip
When investigating media issues always try to refer to specific examples to support your points. Avoid just giving your opinion.

Writing about media issues

TASK

Write an article for a magazine or newspaper about the media issue you have investigated. Remember to set it out like an article and think about how you will attract your audience and make them want to read about the issue.

Media organisations

The media is made up of industries and **organisations** whose purpose is to produce media texts for audiences, for example films and newspapers. Their aim is to make money out of producing these texts. To make sure that what they produce makes a profit, the organisation must **market** and promote themselves and what they produce to an audience.

When you study any media text it is important that you are aware of the organisation that produced it as this will have a role in shaping the text and how that organisation tries to reach its audience.

Marketing and promotion

All media texts are in competition with each other for audiences. The media organisations will constantly think up new ways to attract and maintain audiences. If they don't, then they will not earn money. For the texts you study, you will need to explore the marketing strategies they use. These may include:

- The use of stars and celebrities to market texts.
- Cross-media campaigns, for example advertising television programmes on a radio station.
- Researching audiences to find out what they like and want.
- Strategies used against competition. For example, television organisations think carefully about when they will schedule a programme so that it will gain the highest ratings.

Regulation

Media organisations are not free to do what they want. They have to follow certain rules to make sure that audiences are protected. Most media industries are controlled by outside agencies that check that they are acting responsibly. The organisations also regulate themselves; for example, television companies use the watershed of 9pm to tell audiences when programmes may be less suitable for children, after this time audiences know that programmes may contain stronger language and violence, for example. CDs display 'parental advisory' stickers on the front.

Key Terms

Media organisations
These are the industries and groups that make up the media as a whole, for example television channels, magazine publishers and film companies.

Marketing
This is the way in which the organisation tells its audience about a product. It will use different ways in order to do this, for example a film company will produce trailers and posters to promote a new film. It will also make sure that the stars appear on chat shows and give interviews just before the release of the film.

Regulation
These are the rules that control what the media organisation can and can't include in what they produce.

Regulation

TASK

Find out which of the following regulatory bodies is responsible for controlling which media industry:

Key Terms

Flagship
This is a programme that is important to the channel as it is popular and audiences recognise it as belonging to the channel, for example *EastEnders* for BBC1.

Dumbing down
This term refers to the fact that some people think that television programmes are not challenging and that audiences are 'couch potatoes' who just want programmes that are easy to watch.

Independent research

Choose a media organisation or industry to research, for example television, magazines, music, etc.

Find out information about:

- How the media industry makes money.
- How it is organised.
- Successful examples from the industry, e.g. **flagship** television programmes.
- Any issues associated with the industry, e.g. the '**dumbing down**' of television, film certification, games regulation, etc.
- Stars/personalities associated with the industry.
- How the media industry markets and promotes itself and its products.

TASK

Why is it difficult to regulate the Internet? How do you think this may be done?

Research presentation

Make a display or a PowerPoint presentation of your key findings. Think about how to make your presentation interesting for your audience:

- Do not cut and paste chunks of information from websites. Read the information first and then break it down into easy to understand points.
- Use your own words. If you understand what you are saying then so will your audience.
- Do not have too much information to read on your slides, this will put off your audience.
- Make your presentation interesting to look at, include images and video extracts to illustrate your points and to hold the attention of your audience.
- Involve your audience by asking them questions or inviting their opinions.

2: Introduction to the Media Studies Framework

The Media Studies Framework is made up of the key areas that you must cover when you are exploring any media topics. The framework can be applied to all media texts and will help you to investigate them in detail. Understanding the elements that make up the framework will prepare you for the GCSE external examination and the controlled assessment. The separate parts of this framework were explored in more detail in the previous section. The framework includes:

Media texts

- **Genre** – the codes and conventions that place texts in recognisable genres and sub-genres.
- **Narrative** – the way in which different narratives are constructed.
- Representation – the way groups of people, issues and events are presented in different media texts.

Media organisations

- The ways in which different types of media are regulated and controlled in order to protect audiences.
- Why some media organisations, for example the Internet, are difficult to regulate.
- The ways in which media organisations, for example television channels, market and promote themselves to an audience. For example, in 2013, Channel 4 introduced a new **ident** to remind audiences what the channel is about.

Media audiences and users

- The ways in which different media texts target and appeal to audiences.
- The different ways in which audiences can be described and put into categories.
- The different ways in which audiences respond to texts and what affects the way in which they respond.

Now we need to look at this framework in a bit more detail and explore how it can be used to analyse texts across a range of topic areas.

Key Terms

Genre
This is a type of media text that is easily recognisable to audiences.

Narrative
This is the story that is told by the media text.

Ident
This is the way in which the channel can be 'identified'. The ident is a short image that works as a logo for the channel. It usually appears before the programmes, for example the animated '2' of BBC2.

New Channel 4 ident

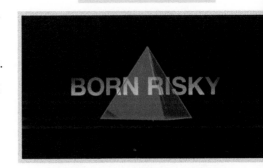

Tip
You will find more detailed information about media organisations in Section 1 What is the Media?

Exploring genre

Genre is the type or category of a media product, for example a music magazine, a horror film or a television news programme. Each genre has its own set of **conventions** that make up the text and that are familiar to its audience. These conventions are recognised and understood by the audience because they are repeated over a period of time. Genres have names, for example soap opera, western, action film, etc. Some styles of media texts cut across more than one genre, for example a romantic comedy or rom-com, and are termed **hybrid texts**.

The conventions of any genre can be broken down into key areas.

Narrative

Plot – how the story is told. All media texts communicate information to their audiences through a clear structure. Films (and some television programmes) may use a linear structure where the events follow one after another and include a beginning, middle and an ending. An audience will then know what to expect from the narrative of certain texts.

Plot situations – these are predictable and recognisable storylines or scenes within the narrative of a specific genre, for example in a reality television show like *I'm a Celebrity Get Me out of Here* we expect to see some sort of trial or task which the celebrities must undertake.

Characters – each genre has a recognisable set of characters. Audiences will be used to these character types and will anticipate how they will behave in certain situations. Some genres will represent characters in a particular way, for example women in rap music videos are often represented in a negative way.

Stars – these can be actors that the audience associates with a particular genre or character, for example Daniel Craig as James Bond.

Key Terms

Conventions
What we expect to see in a text belonging to a specific genre.

Hybrid texts
These are media texts that are difficult to place in one particular genre as they have the elements of different genres. For example, the genre of *Dr Who* could be said to be a science fiction/fantasy/drama.

I'm A Celebrity trial

TASK

Choose a television or film genre. Give examples of the plot structure, a plot situation and characters associated with that genre.

Settings and iconography

Typical settings – the **settings** may clearly belong to a particular genre. The wards and offices of *Holby City* are recognisable to audiences as belonging to the hospital drama genre.

Objects – for example, the equipment in a hospital drama. Audiences get used to seeing these objects in texts belonging to the same genre.

Tip
Learning the terminology that will help you to explore genre will help you to complete one of your Textual investigations.

Setting and iconography in *Holby City*

Objects can also be important in print texts; for example, the electric guitar held by a musician on the front cover of *Kerrang!* magazine gives a clue to the magazine's genre.

Clothing – this is a quick way of telling the audience the genre of the text and for giving information about characters. The appearance of a character in a nurse's uniform tells the audience their role in the narrative and the audience have expectations of how they will behave.

Technical codes

Camera shots, angles and movement – these are important in establishing the genre of the text. Certain media texts use particular shots to communicate messages to audiences. Music videos and CD covers will often use close-up shots of the performer with a **direct mode of address** to make it more personal for the audience. In the poster for *Iron Man 3*, the low angle shot makes the character look more powerful.

Special effects – some genres, for example action films, use special effects to make the film more dramatic.

Editing – the way in which the text is put together suggests the genre. Films and television programmes that try to create suspense will use slower editing; the editing of action films will be faster paced.

Choose a different film or television genre. Give examples of typical settings, objects and clothing linked to that genre.

Key Terms

Setting
The time and place where the action takes place in texts like a film, television programme or music video.

Iconography
The props, costumes, objects and backgrounds belonging to a particular genre.

Direct mode of address
In an audio-visual or print text, this means that the subject is looking straight at the audience. This involves the audience more.

Quickfire 6

How does setting help to show the genre of a media text?

Task

Audio codes

Music – an audience will associate certain music with a particular genre; for example, the eerie music in horror films used in order to build tension. Certain instruments suggest a genre, for example violin music in a romantic film.

Sound effects – these are also linked to specific genres. For example, the arrival of Dr Who's Tardis is a very memorable sound effect recognised by a range of audiences.

Dialogue – the speech in an audio-visual text and the language used reflect the genre. In a hospital drama we expect to hear vocabulary linked to medical procedures.

Here is an extract from a script for BBC's hospital drama *Casualty*:

A conversation in *Casualty*

```
JEFF AND HIS N/S PARAMEDIC RUSH IN WITH WILLIAM ON A
TROLLEY. THEY ARE TALKING TO MAGGIE, CHARLIE AND RUTH.
WILLIAM IS NOW CRYING. HE'S ON OXYGEN AND HAS HIS RIGHT
LEG AND ARM IN A FRAC PACK. CHARLIE REASSURES HIM.

                        CHARLIE

            You're alright. My name's Charlie.

                         JEFF

        This is William. He's eight. Possible fracture of
        radius/ulna of the right arm. Fractured tib and fib.
           2.4ml of morphine for the pain. GCS 15 on scene.

THEY GO INTO PAEDS RESUS

                     JEFF (CONT'D)

               On my count, one, two, three.

WILLIAM CRIES OUT IN PAIN

                        MAGGIE

               Let's get another line put in.

                         JEFF

        He had some Entonox on the way in. He's been a very
                         brave boy.
```

How do we know this is a script from a medical drama?

Tip

Listen to the type of music used in films and television programmes. When is it used and why? What is the effect on the audience? Try to avoid just saying 'the music is loud', mention the instruments that make it loud and the pace. Is it loud throughout the scene or does it build up to match the dramatic action?

Independent research

Go to The Writers' Room on the BBC website: www.bbc.co.uk/writersroom/. Here you can look at scripts from a range of different television genres and develop your understanding of how dialogue helps to suggest genre. Notice how the scripts are set out, this is important and you will need to do this if you produce a script for your production work.

Exploring narrative

Narrative is another important part of the Media Studies Framework. It is linked to the genre of the text as mentioned previously, but it is important to explore it separately. Whatever topic you study, you will investigate how it is structured and put together. All media texts tell stories, both factual and fictional. Narrative in Media Studies is a little different in meaning from other subjects like English. In Media Studies it means the way in which any text unfolds its information to an audience. For example, a women's magazine has an obvious front cover followed by a contents page, horoscopes tend to be towards the back and there is usually an advert on the back cover. Regular readers are used to the structure and know where to find things.

Linear narratives – this way of structuring stories was noticed by the theorist Todorov during his research into fairy tales and traditional stories. He discovered that narratives moved forward in a **chronological** order with one action following after another. There was a clear beginning, middle and an end. He also discovered that the characters involved in the narrative would be changed in some way by the end.

Non-linear/circular narratives – in this structure the narrative may move backwards and forwards in time or in a circular narrative beginning at the end of the story. Techniques such as flashbacks may be used. However, some genres use a non-linear narrative structure regularly, for example sports programmes like *Match of The Day* move backwards and forwards from the live studio to the matches played earlier that day.

Media texts use a range of narrative techniques to hold the attention of the audience. Some narratives have several narrative strands and the audience has to work harder to understand what is happening. Codes, for example flashbacks and **enigmas**, also make the text more interesting.

In Section 5: Television Crime Drama you will see how narrative can be explored in more detail in a specific topic.

Key Terms

Chronological
This is a narrative where the events are shown in the order in which they happened from beginning to end.

Enigmas
These are mysteries or puzzles in the narrative. Enigmas keep an audience interested in the story.

TASK

What is the structure of the following media texts?

1. A newspaper
2. A CD cover
3. A music video
4. A television news programme
5. A romantic comedy

TASK

Think of an example of a text that uses a linear narrative and one that uses a non-linear narrative.

Exploring representation

Key Terms

Representation
How people, places, issues and events are presented in different media texts in order to create meanings.

Digitally enhanced
This means that an image is changed on a computer. For example, a computer program can lengthen the neck of the model, get rid of marks on his/her face, make them thinner, straighten their nose, etc.

Stereotypes
This is where a group of people are shown in a particular way by exaggerating certain characteristics.

This is another important element of Media Studies and it is quite complex. The media is not a 'window on the world', by this we mean that it does not show the real world, it shows us a version of it that has been represented according to the type of text.

In order to help you to analyse the **representations** in a range of media texts you will need to understand that:

- All media texts are constructed. For example, a model on the front of a magazine may be airbrushed and **digitally enhanced**; he/she will not look the same as if we saw them in 'real life'. Technical codes and editing in audio-visual texts is another way in which representations are constructed. For example, taking a photograph of a group of teenagers using low key lighting for a film poster may make them look more dangerous.

- Below is an example of an image of actress Rachel Weisz that has clearly been digitally enhanced to be used in an anti-wrinkle cream advert. The advertisement was banned because it was seen to be misleading for audiences.

Spot the difference?

- Media texts use **stereotypes** to give out messages quickly to an audience. Stereotypes work by over-emphasising certain features of a person, for example the moodiness and unreasonable behaviour of a teenager. The audience will recognise certain stereotypes and know how they will behave. For example, the cheeky teenager in a soap opera, or the career woman in an advertisement. Not all stereotypes are negative. 'Irish people are friendly' is an example of a positive stereotype.

- Different audiences will respond to representations in different ways. For example, teenagers may be unhappy about the way in which they are represented in some national newspapers.

- In Section 7: Lifestyle and Celebrity you will find more information on representation in a specific media topic.

Give an example of how a stereotype can be used to communicate a message quickly.

Consider how women and young people are represented in these two texts

Technical codes and digital enhancing have been used in this advert. The model's skin is perfect, there are no shadows, lines or blemishes. This is an unrealistic representation of a woman.

High key lighting has been used to make her look even more perfect.

The blue of her eyes has been made brighter and more shiny

Her eyelashes have been made longer digitally in order to persuade the audience that the mascara did this. They may then buy the product.

In this film poster the aim is to make the young people look dangerous and intimidating. This has been done through:

Technical codes – the lighting is low key and there are shadows on faces to give clues to characters.

Visual codes – the colours are muted giving the poster a more urban feel to it. There are also suggestions of an urban setting.

Iconography – the clothing is typical of city teenagers and the use of the hoodie suggests a stereotype audiences will recognise. The baseball bat suggests violence will be an element of the film.

Mode of address – the characters are looking directly at the audience and their expressions are challenging and a bit scary.

Key Term

High key lighting
Bright lighting usually used to emphasise certain aspects of a scene or image.

Task

Find examples of media texts that represent gender (men or women) or age (young or old) people) in different ways. Explore how these representations have been constructed and the effect they may have on an audience.

Audience

It is impossible to explore a media text without considering the audience for the text. Every media text has a **target audience** and texts such as films, music videos and magazines will work hard to attract their audience in order to be successful.

How do media texts target and appeal to an audience?

Different texts use different methods. Some media texts aim to attract a broad audience, other texts, for example specialised magazines, attract a smaller, **niche audience**. Some television programmes will use **narrow casting** to appeal to a specific, smaller audience; this is the opposite of **broadcasting**. Methods may include:

● **Technical and audio codes** – film trailers for action films, for example, will use fast editing and dramatic music to appeal to the audience. The trailer will also usually be shown before a film of a similar genre so that the right audience is targeted. Within a film or television programme the type of shots will involve the audience and make the text more interesting to watch.

● **Layout and design** – the front pages of gossip magazines like *OK!* and *heat* are very busy and use lots of images, colour and dramatic headlines in order to persuade the reader to buy.

● **Language and mode of address** – some magazines will often use a chatty, informal style so that the reader feels like they are talking directly to them about their lives. They may also use vocabulary that only an audience interested in the magazine's topic would understand. This makes the reader feel exclusive and special.

TASK

Explore how the following three media texts: a web page, a magazine and a film poster target and appeal to their audience.

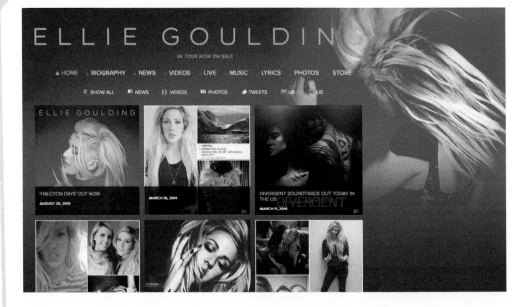

QUICKfire 9

Why is it important that a text successfully appeals to its audience?

Tip

Think about the range of different audiences that the texts may appeal to.

PlayStation.
Official Magazine - UK
Issue 094 June 2013 £5.99
officialplaystationmagazine.co.uk

EVERY BIG
PS3 GAME!
METAL GEAR SOLID V:
THE PHANTOM PAIN
CASTLEVANIA:
LORDS OF SHADOW 2
THE LAST OF US
GTA V

BATMAN
ARKHAM ORIGINS
The Dark Knight returns
– and this time he's
in Gotham!

PS4 EXCLUSIVE
KILLZONE
SHADOW FALL
The new generation of shooters starts here

DIABLO III
Hands-on with PS4's
darkest, deepest RPG

SAINTS ROW IV TEARAWAY METRO: LAST LIGHT THIEF

Quickfire
10

How do we know
if a text has been
successful in
appealing to an
audience?

Now choose a media text of your own. Explore it showing how it has attempted to appeal to its target audience.

Task

What affects the way in which an audience responds to a media text?

Media texts work hard to appeal to their target audience. If they don't, they won't make a profit. However, not all audiences will respond to media texts in the same way. In the media habits section on page 10, you will have learned that different people like different media texts for different reasons. These include:

Is it only older people who are less likely to play computer games?

Some older people may enjoy playing computer games

- Gender – men and women like different texts. In general, some women like gossip magazines as they tend to be more interested than men in the lives of celebrities.

- Age – people of different ages like different texts. Older people may be less happy with a film that includes lots of violence and bad language. They may also be less likely to play computer games as their generation was not brought up with this type of media. This is a generalisation and you may know older people who like and use these texts.

- Ethnicity – people from different cultural backgrounds often have different ideas and beliefs and this may affect their response to a text. An Asian audience may be unhappy with the way that they are represented in a programme like *Citizen Khan*, for example.

- Situation – where you are and who you are with has an effect on how you respond to a text. You may enjoy a film more if you see it in the cinema than if you watch it on the television at home. You may laugh more at a comedy programme if you are watching it with your friends rather than on your own.

> **TASK**
> Think of some other specific examples of how age and gender can affect how an audience may respond to a text.

How and why do audiences consume media texts?

There are lots of theories about how and why audiences use certain media texts. These have changed over time as media texts have changed and developed. Audiences tend to be active now and make choices about the texts they consume. This is often referred to as the **uses and gratifications theory** and it is the most useful one to refer to when exploring the choices audiences make. It suggested that audiences have different needs and will choose texts that satisfy these needs. They use texts for:

- Entertainment and diversion – audiences like to escape from their everyday lives by consuming texts that are entertaining.

- Information and education – some texts give us information about what is going on in the world and therefore educate and inform us. For example, news programmes, newspapers and television documentaries. Even fictional texts can inform us, for example a costume drama like *Downton Abbey* gives us information about how people lived at that time.

- Social interaction – some texts are talking points and are discussed by people as they happen. For example, who will win *The X Factor*, or what is happening in *I'm a Celebrity Get Me Out of Here*.

- Personal identity – some audiences like to watch or read texts because they can compare their lives and experiences with those featured in the text. For example, a storyline in a soap or an article in a magazine.

Complete the following table giving examples of texts that audiences consume for different reasons. Try to ensure that your examples cover a range of media platforms, don't just use examples of films.

Audience need	Example of text
Entertainment and diversion	
Information and education	
Social interaction	
Personal identity	

Key Terms

Social interaction
Talking to people about a particular subject.

Personal identity
This means your ability to relate to something that happens in a text because it has happened to you.

Reading
In Media Studies this refers to your understanding of the text.

How do audiences respond to texts?

Audiences do not all respond to texts in the same way, as we have said earlier, lots of different factors affect how we feel about certain media texts. Media texts give out messages to an audience; for example, some magazines tell us how we should look, what we should be wearing and what we should spend our money on. Some audiences will agree with these messages and some will not. Stuart Hall, a media theorist, explored how audiences respond to texts and he said there are three different ways in which we might 'read' a media text:

The preferred reading – this is where the audience agrees with what the text is telling them. So, the reader of *Men's Fitness* magazine will accept that he should really look like the man on the cover and he will try to follow the advice of the magazine to improve his body image.

The negotiated reading – here the audience will accept some of the messages contained within the text, but will ignore others. For example, he may try some of the exercises in the magazine in an attempt to get fit, but accepts he will never look like the man on the cover!

The oppositional reading – here an audience will not agree at all with the messages in the text. This may be the man who does not feel the need to look like a *Men's Fitness* man and therefore would not even buy the magazine!

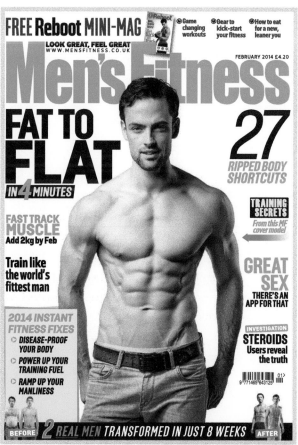

QUICKFIRE 12

How could you apply the uses and gratifications theory to your own media consumption?

Key Figure
Stuart Hall is a media theorist who investigated how people make sense of media texts. He suggested that producers of media texts had an idea of how audiences should respond to their texts but that audiences would often respond differently for a range of different reasons.

Why might an audience have an oppositional reading of a text?

Other responses?

Theories are important but so are actual responses from audiences. These can be found in:

- Audience ratings for television programmes.
- Blogs on websites for films, magazines and other texts where audiences can give their opinions.
- Film reviews.
- Box office numbers showing how many people actually went to see the film.
- Sales figures for newspapers.
- 'Hits' for websites.

Independent research

Choose a specific media text, for example a recent film or television programme. Try to find a range of actual audience responses to this text.

3: A Toolkit for Analysis

It is important that during the course you develop the skills to investigate any print, audio-visual or interactive media text. To do this you will need to look at lots of different media texts and to develop your media vocabulary. This will be your '**Toolkit**', it will help you to understand the text and to discuss it using the correct terminology. You will then be able to transfer your knowledge and understanding to any text you are asked to study. Exploring a range of texts will also prepare you for planning and creating your own.

Each type of media text also has a **language** that is unique. You need to be aware of the language that is specific to the text that you are investigating; this will become part of your 'Toolkit'.

What is a sign?

A sign is something that sends out meanings to an audience. It can be a word or an image.

What is a code?

One of the ways in which media texts communicate messages is through codes; these are systems of signs, for example technical and visual codes. Audiences recognise and understand the **connotations** of the codes in a media text. Every media text has a range of meanings that will be understood by audiences.

Key Terms

Toolkit
The set of key points that you must refer to when you are exploring a specific media text.

Language
The words used in a media text that may give a clue to its genre. For example, the medical terms used in a programme like *Casualty*.

Connotations
The meanings attached to the sign, for example the use of the colour blue in an advert for toothpaste suggests freshness and cleanliness.

Find some examples of signs that communicate meanings to audiences. Annotate your examples to show how the sign contains meanings. Here are some examples. Consider how the meaning of the sign changes according to where you see it.

TASK

Tip
Consider how you will use your understanding of how signs and codes work to help you to explore media texts.

27

Visual codes

Visual codes are what we see in a media text and how we, as the audience, may interpret them. All media texts have meanings **encoded** in them and audiences **decode** them. We interpret signs and codes around us in our everyday life; we just need to be able to transfer that understanding to analysing the media.

- **Code of clothing** – clothing communicates messages about people. In the media, as in daily life, we make decisions about people according to what they are wearing. Clothing is a rapid way of telling the audience about a person, this may be the way a person has decided to dress themselves, for example a music star, or how a director has constructed them, for example a character in a film or television programme.

- **Code of expression** – facial expressions quickly communicate messages about how someone is feeling. For this reason the producers of media texts often use close-ups of faces to show emotion.

- **Codes of gesture** – gestures are effective **non-verbal communicators**. For example, the way a band or artist uses body language on the front cover of a CD or on their website may effectively give out messages about their style of music or their attitude.

- **Codes of colour** – colours have meanings. Advertisements, for example, use colour to suggest something about their product – cereal advertisements will often use bright yellow colours to make the audience feel that the product will make us feel happy and healthy.

QuickFire 14

Give three examples of how clothing can convey a message.

Task

How does the CD cover design for Black Veil Brides' *Set the World on Fire* use visual codes to convey meanings to an audience?

- **Code of technique** – this refers to the way in which an image may be manipulated in order to convey messages. For example, enhancing the redness and glossiness of the lipstick on a model's lips in an advertisement.
- **Iconography** – the objects, settings and backgrounds used in a media text contain meanings. We recognise some genres instantly because of their iconography.
- **Graphics** – the choice of font style and other drawings or CGI images will communicate messages about the text.
- **Images** – the images in any media text will have been carefully chosen. The way they will have been constructed and positioned within the text will also have meaning, for example the construction of a film poster where it is important that the producers of the text communicate messages about the film's genre, storyline and characters.

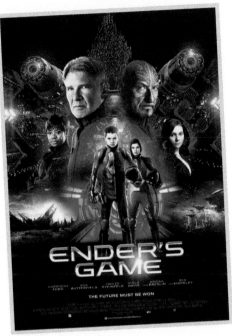

QUICKFIRE
15

How do the images convey meaning in the film poster for *Ender's Game*?

Analysing audio-visual media texts

In exploring **audio-visual texts**, for example television extracts, trailers and television advertisements, you must be able to pick out the main **technical codes** that have been used to construct the text and to investigate their purpose and effect. Technical codes can be divided into:

- Camera shots
- Camera angles
- Camera movement
- Editing.

Camera shots

A media text is constructed using a range of different shots to create a particular effect. There are a lot of different types of shot and it is important for all aspects of this course that you can use the correct terminology to discuss the way in which they are employed. Some of the most useful include the following.

Give another example of when a media text may use an extreme close-up. Remember to consider the purpose and **effect** of the shot.

The close-up

As the name suggests, this shot gives us detail, it positions the audience close to the subject. This may be to make us feel involved in what is happening with a character, for example if they are upset, or to emphasise the importance of an object – here the message on a mobile phone in a television drama.

The extreme close-up

This shot gives a limited amount of detail and focuses on a particular aspect of the subject. For example, the eyes of a character who is scared in a horror film, or to show the effectiveness of a particular product in an advertisement, for example red lipstick.

The medium shot

This is also called the 'newsreader' shot as it frames a subject from head to waist as seen in the shot of a news anchor; it gives a little more information than a close-up shot.

The long shot

This gives the audience even more information and has a different **purpose**. The shot will usually include a person or object and something around them to give a clue to where they are.

The establishing shot

This shot is used to communicate information quickly to an audience about where the action is about to take place. If the audience recognises the location, they may have expectations of what will happen next. For example, a shot of the front of The Queen Vic in *EastEnders* tells the audience that this is a communal meeting place for a range of characters in this soap opera; they know the next shot will take them inside and continue the narrative.

Camera angles

Where the camera is placed in relation to the subject can affect how that subject is viewed and understood by an audience. Shots, angles and camera movement are edited together to create a narrative, just like a story is put together by words and sentences to convey meaning.

High angle shots

Filming a character from a high angle will have the effect of making that character appear vulnerable, weak or scared. Other types of high angle shots are **bird's eye view shot** or aerial shot and a **crane shot**.

A camera mounted on a crane to film a high angle shot

Low angle shots

Filming a character or object from a low angle makes the subject appear more intimidating and powerful to the audience. Low angle shots are also sometimes used to make smaller actors, for example Tom Cruise, appear more dominant in a scene. If the subject is filmed with sky or another expanse of space as a background it will make them appear even more forceful to an audience. Other types of low angle shots include a worm's eye shot where the camera is at ground level.

Russell Crowe as Maximus in *Gladiator*, framed in a low angle shot to appear heroic

Eye level

This angle is straight on to the subject matter, the audience will view the scene or character as if they were looking at it through their own eyes, in this way it is a more realistic depiction of the action.

Hannibal in *Silence of the Lambs*

Canted angle

In this shot the camera is tilted at an oblique angle, its purpose being to disorientate an audience. This is often combined with a **point of view shot** to involve the audience in the action as a particular character and is a popular technique used in the horror genre.

A canted angle disorientates the audience

Key Terms

Bird's eye view shot
This where a scene is shot from overhead. This is often used to film car chases, for example. It allows a lot of the scene to be shown at once but not in any detail.

Crane shot
This shot is not as extreme as an aerial shot; here the camera is elevated above the action using a crane.

Point of view shot
This where the camera shows the audience the action through the eyes of a character. This makes them feel more involved.

Tip

Becoming familiar with the filming techniques used by professional film-makers will enable you to make your own audio-visual texts more effective.

Camera movement

The way in which the camera moves within an audio-visual sequence can develop the narrative and engage the attention of the audience. The style of the movement will be chosen to suit the specific sequence. The main camera movements are as follows.

Tracking shots

This is the term for when the camera follows a character or the action, the purpose is to make the audience feel involved in what is happening. A reverse track is when the camera moves back as the character or objects move towards the camera.

A zoom

Here the focus changes from a long shot to a close-up of the character or object. The zoom is a subtle shot and should not be noticed by the audience. A good example is when the camera zooms in to focus on a character's face for a **reaction shot** in an argument. The purpose of a zoom is to give the audience more detail and involve them in what is happening emotionally.

A pan

In this shot the camera moves across the screen horizontally, it may be used to show a crowd scene or a landscape. If this is done at speed it is a whip pan and is used to suggest panic and pace.

A tilt

In this shot the camera moves vertically up or down the screen. It is often used to withhold information from an audience, for example introducing a character by focusing on their feet first.

Key Term

Reaction shot
This is a shot that cuts away from the main scene in the film to show the reaction of a particular character to what has happened. It is commonly used to show an emotional response to something that has happened or has been said.

Tip

Avoid just describing what the camera does. In Section A of the examination you may be required to explain how or why specific technical codes have been used.

TASK

Using the table headings below, consider when certain shots, angles and movements may be used in an audio-visual media text and their purpose and effect.

	Media text	Purpose	Effect
Close-up			
Establishing shot			
High angle			
Tracking shot			

Audio codes

When analysing audio-visual texts you must not forget about sound! Many students fail to listen carefully to the sound included in a text and to consider why it has been chosen and its possible effect on an audience. Just as with exploring camera techniques, there is a range of media terminology appropriate when investigating **audio codes** in a media text.

All sound can be referred to as **diegetic** or **non-diegetic sound**. The different types of audio codes you may expect to hear in an audio-visual text are:

- Music – this audio code can very rapidly convey information to the audience about what is happening or how they should feel. An audience may expect certain types of music when they are watching a particular film or television genre.

- Sound effects – these make an audio-visual text more true to life. They can also be used to add excitement and tension, for example an explosion in an action film. In some media texts the sound effects are made louder for effect, for example the noise of an engine in a television advertisement for a performance car.

- Dialogue – what characters say and how they say it is an important way in which information is conveyed to audiences in audio-visual texts. The language used in the dialogue can also give clues to the genre of the text. For example, the technical medical terminology used in *Casualty* places it in the sub-genre of hospital drama and adds to the programme's realism.

- Voice-overs – some texts use a non-diegetic voice that gives information to the audience. This technique is most commonly used in film trailers and advertisements and can also be a persuasive device.

Give a specific example of how music can communicate messages to an audience.

Analysing print texts

Examples of print texts include film posters, magazines, comics, CD and DVD covers. Like audio-visual texts, print texts also have their own language 'Toolkit' that you will have to learn and apply in order to discuss examples in a sophisticated way. As with audio-visual texts, the more practice you get and the more you are aware of the different print texts that are around, the better will become your ability to explore them in detail. In the later sections of this book you will learn in more detail about specific texts, what follows is a general overview.

Technical and visual codes in print texts

- **Layout and design** – the decisions made by the producers of a print text about how the text will be constructed are very important in attracting an audience. The selection and placing of images, the choice of typography, and the use of colour are part of the layout and design and contribute to the overall appeal of the text.

- **Camera shots and angles** – these aspects are equally as important in a print text as in an audio-visual one. Magazines may choose to present their cover model in a close-up or long shot according to the message they want to convey to the reader. For example, a low angle shot of a character on the front cover of a film magazine may make them seem more dominant and intimidating.

- **Visual codes** – colour, expression, gesture and clothing all work together in the construction of messages in a print text.

- **Codes of technique** – print texts are often changed as part of the **post-production** process. This may involve techniques like heightening colours, adding CGI effects and airbrushing.

Key Term

Post-production
This is the term for any production work that takes place on moving or still images after the initial filming or photography shoot has taken place.

Task

What decisions have been made about technical and visual codes in the construction of the front cover for *Total Film* magazine?

Quickfire 18

Why do media texts like magazines and print advertisements use airbrushing effects?

Language and mode of address

It is important when analysing a media text to consider how it 'speaks' to its audience. This means the language used and the style of presentation. When analysing language, as with other aspects of the media, you need to use the relevant terminology. For all texts, the words used within them have been carefully selected to send the right messages to the audience. These include:

- **Lexis** – this term refers to the specific words that are used. Subject-specific lexis will help to attract the right audience. The language on this *PlayStation Magazine* is only understandable and relevant to the specific target audience.

- **Hyperbole** – this is over-exaggerated language used to create an effect or be persuasive, for example, in advertisements.
- **Direct quotations** – these make the story in a magazine seem more believable.

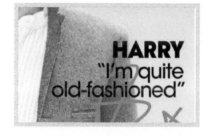

- **Slang or colloquial language** – in magazines for young people this helps to engage the young audience.
- **The imperative** – this is a statement that gives an order, it is usually accompanied by an exclamation mark, it encourages the audience to take action and suggests the importance of what is being said.

- **Mode of address** – this is the tone of the written or spoken language. There are different types of **mode of address**: **formal**, **informal**, **direct** and **indirect**. Different texts will use different styles according to their target audience.

TASK

Create a front page of a new magazine aimed at young people. Use as many of the above language devices as you can on your front cover. Label the cover using the appropriate terminology showing what impact the language and mode of address would have on the target audience.

Analysing media texts: putting it all together

Consider how what you have learned about analysing media texts can be applied to a specific example like the one here.

Visual codes

The **colour** black and the style of leather clothing suggest the glam metal music genre. The **iconography** of tattoos, piercing and make-up also reinforces this. The paper held by the lead singer has the readers' questions on it and links to the sub-heading, it also suggests the readers of the magazine have had exclusive access to this band. The **code of expression** of the band is challenging and suggests an attitude, the high chins conveying arrogance. **The mode of address** is direct and engages the audience. The images on the free posters also use a direct mode of address.

Language

Hyperbole is used: *the most controversial band in the universe* and reinforces the band's representation. The use of the **direct quotation** encourages the reader to buy the magazine. There is also **subject-specific lexis** in that the names of the bands will only be known to those familiar with the genre.

Technical codes

The eye level camera angle used for the main image involves the audience.

Layout and design

There is a strong **central image** which also establishes a hierarchy within the band. The layout of the text is unconventional – the headline is placed at an angle and there is a range of different fonts including a handwritten style. The **font style** of *Kerrang!* is bold and assertive, this suggests a rebellious non-conformist magazine aimed at young people.

Task

Choose a text and annotate it showing your ability to apply your knowledge and understanding of how to analyse a text.

4: What is a Topic?

The Media Studies GCSE will be taught through topics. Some topics will be chosen by your teachers, others will be set for you by the Awarding Body (WJEC). Topics are areas of the media that may cover more than one **media form**. For example, Science Fiction is a topic and you can investigate texts linked to this topic in television, radio, film, magazines and comics. In this way you can explore how different media platforms link together and support each other. Other topics may include:

- Advertising and Marketing
- Lifestyle and Celebrity
- Drama
- Animation
- News
- Music

Each topic you study will give you the opportunity to explore examples of media texts from different platforms and to create your own media texts.

For the GCSE examination, one topic will be set and you will be told which elements of the topic will be the focus for the two sections of the examination paper. For example, the topic set for 2015 is Advertising and Marketing. Section A is Print Advertising and Section B is Television Advertising.

Key Term

Media form
This is a range of different ways of communicating including the Internet, television and newspapers.

How is the topic of 'Drama' presented across different media platforms?

It is important to be prepared for the examination

Tip

Understanding the structure of the examination paper and what is expected of you in the different sections will help you to prepare.

The Examination: Thinking about the Media: Investigating and Planning

This is 40% of your final mark at GCSE.

Section A: Thinking about the Media – Investigating

You will respond to some **stimulus material** linked to the examination topic, for example in 2015 this may be adverts from magazines. This material can be print or audio-visual depending on the set topic. This section will allow you to demonstrate your knowledge of the topic (print advertising), your ability to investigate texts and your knowledge of media terminology. The later questions will assess your knowledge and understanding of the Media Studies Framework.

If an audio-visual extract is set for Section A you will be shown it three times.

- You will have 5 minutes at the beginning of the exam to read the questions before you see the extract.
- For the first viewing you just watch.
- For the second viewing you can make notes.
- You will then be given 10 minutes for further note-taking; the time will count down on the screen.
- You will then see the extract for a third and final time when you can check and add to your notes.

If print is the topic for Section A you will keep the stimulus material for the whole examination, but you must still give yourself time to think about the questions and to make notes about the print stimulus material before you start to answer the questions.

Questions 1 and 2 will usually be related to the stimulus material you are shown and will assess aspects of the Media Studies Framework. Use the mark allocation as a guide. You may be asked to comment on:

- Camera shots and angles.
- Editing.
- Audio codes.
- Genre conventions, for example setting, narrative, characters, etc.
- Visual codes – iconography, gesture, expression, clothing, colour, etc.
- Layout and design.

Examples of Questions 1 and 2

The set topic here was Television Drama. The stimulus material was an extract from ITV's *Downton Abbey*.

1. (a) Identify two different settings used in the extract.   [4]

   (b) Briefly explain why these two settings were used.   [6]

Key Term

Stimulus material
These are the resources you will be given and asked to respond to in Section A of the examination. They may be audio-visual, for example an extract from a television crime drama, or print, for example two print advertisements depending on the set topic.

Tip

Try to analyse your examples in detail using media vocabulary. Avoid description.

2. (a) Identify two different storylines in the extract. [4]

   (b) Briefly explain how each of the storylines appeals to audiences. [6]

The paper has to allow all students to attempt the questions but it also has to challenge students.

Questions 3 and 4 you may find more difficult; they will ask you to discuss broader areas related to the set topic, for example:

- Representation: for example age, gender.
- Narrative structures.
- The ways in which the texts are promoted and marketed.
- Why the texts are popular with an audience.
- Why they are important to channels/TV companies/other organisations?
- How the texts target and appeal to audiences.

You must include specific examples from the examination topic in these more demanding questions. You should refer to your own examples that you have studied in class in your response.

Examples of Questions 3 and 4

3. Explain how age is represented in one Television Drama you have studied. [10]

4. Explain why Television Drama continues to be popular with audiences. [10]

Section B: Thinking about the Media – Planning

In this section you will demonstrate your ability to plan and create through a series of tasks which allow you to demonstrate your knowledge about the media.

You will be asked to complete tasks linked to planning/ creating a media text, for example ideas for a television advertisement for a new product. You may be asked to design a logo or create a storyboard for a new advert.

You will be asked to justify the decisions you have made. Make sure that you show your understanding of the conventions of the text you have created. Learn and use relevant vocabulary.

This section allows you to demonstrate your knowledge and understanding of the codes and conventions of a media text.

You will be given opportunities to practise for this task in class during the year.

Task 5 you may find more challenging as it will test your broader understanding of the topic area. It may link to how the texts you have been asked to create appeal to audiences or are important to organisations.

Controlled Assessment

Creating for the Media: Investigating and Producing

This is 60% of your final mark at GCSE.

You will complete an assessment file that must contain **three** pieces of work from **three different media topics and three different media forms.** By the end of the GCSE course you will have in your file:

Two Textual investigations of 400–850 words based on two different media topics and two different media forms. 20%.

- One must be print based.
- One must be based on genre.
- One must be based on narrative or representation

The titles of your Textual investigations are set for you.

In the next sections of this book you will explore topic areas and see examples of possible Textual investigations and how to approach them.

One media production consisting of: 40%.

- Research.
- Planning.
- The actual production piece.
- An evaluation.

You will select your production piece from a range of options given by your teacher including print and moving image. It will be completed over 10/12 weeks, usually in Year 11. During Year 10 you will have completed practice assignments linked to research, planning and pre-production to help you to prepare for this assignment. You will also have learned how to use the equipment required to create your production.

The production piece must not be linked to the examination topic.

Later on in this book there is a section dealing with the Production element of the Controlled Assessment.

5: Television Crime Drama

This is the set topic for **Section A** of the 2014 GCSE examination paper. For this section you will:

- Be shown an extract from a television crime drama three times.

- Answer questions related to this extract. These questions may focus on: technical codes, audio codes, setting, iconography, characters or any other generic conventions.

- Answer broader questions related to the crime drama topic and the Media Studies Framework using examples from the television crime dramas you have studied in class and demonstrating your understanding.

What is television crime drama?

Television crime drama is a **sub-genre** of television drama, which is usually about the committing and solving of a crime. The crime may be solved by a whole range of different types of investigators. The stories in television crime dramas often show what happens in real life. The best television crime dramas keep the audience interested because we believe in the characters and the worlds they create, even if those worlds and characters seem unrealistic. The key features of the **genre** are **characters**, **setting** and **narrative**.

Key Terms

Genre
This is the type of media text, for example a television crime drama. The genre is recognisable by having a set of shared characteristics that audiences expect to see. These are the genre conventions.

Sub-genre
Within the overall genre of television crime drama there will be groups of programmes that share similar conventions, for example detective-led dramas. These are sub-genres.

Hybrid genre
Some programmes share the conventions of more than one genre. *Jonathan Creek* is a crime drama with elements of the paranormal.

Genres, sub-genres and hybrid genres

TASK

Make a list of all the television crime dramas you can think of, past and present.

Now try and divide these programmes into those that share the same conventions and that are different from the others. Give your separate lists a sub-genre title, for example private detective, forensic.

Some of your examples may be defined by when they appear on the television – they may be 'one-off' dramas.

Formats and sub-genres

Crime drama is one of the earliest television genres and it is a genre that has changed and reinvented itself as society and audience expectations have changed. Crime Drama is an 'umbrella' genre with many sub-genres:

Traditional crime drama – this has its roots in the early examples of the genre. Its central characters are a small number of detectives who always solve the crime. This is their main aim and the settings and narrative are related to the crime and the police station. The private lives of the detectives rarely feature. The modern versions of this sub-genre have developed to include more three-dimensional characters and show their lives outside the police station to create realism, e.g. *Scott & Bailey*.

Tip

Learn to recognise the main conventions of the different sub-genres. This will help you to analyse the stimulus material in the examination.

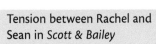

Tension between Rachel and Sean in *Scott & Bailey*

Detective-led crime dramas – these focus on one main character or a detective and a sidekick. Often detectives are slightly unconventional in the way they solve crimes and do not always do things by the book. They tend to be a bit mysterious and the audience becomes intrigued by them and their behaviour.

The team – these sub-genres feature a group of detectives, mainly plain clothes, who deal with the crimes. The narratives tend to extend beyond the crime and may include relationships between the members of the team. Individuals may have a particular specialism, for example Calleigh in *CSI: Miami* is a ballistics expert.

How might a 'team' crime drama attract a wider audience?

Calleigh in action in *CSI: Miami*

Forensic crime dramas – the focus here is on solving the crime through the collection and analysis of evidence. The iconography is usually very hi-tech and this is used to solve the crime rather than traditional police procedures. *Silent Witness* is an example of this sub-genre.

Private detectives – these are investigators working outside of the police although they will sometimes use them, e.g. *Case Histories*. These sub-genres have produced some memorable characters, e.g. Miss Marple, Jackson Brodie in *Case Histories* and Jessica Fletcher in *Murder She Wrote*.

Why are crime dramas important to the television industry?

- They are a well-established genre, and audiences have expectations that they will have high production values, a strong narrative, and a good range of characters.

- Long-running crime dramas, e.g. *New Tricks*, establish a loyal audience. This programme was scheduled on a Monday evening and brought in the highest figures for the BBC for the week.

- They can be produced in a range of formats to try to appeal to an audience. For example, series, serial, one-offs and two-parters.

- They are easy for channels to market because of the clear genre codes and conventions. They often have established stars that have become household names and therefore help the marketing of the programme.

- They are usually long – sometimes 2 hours. This means that a channel can ensure that they have an audience for this length of time.

- Channels often create **spin-offs** of a drama that has been successful as they know they will attract an audience. For example, *Lewis* and *Endeavour* were both inspired by *Inspector Morse*.

- They are exportable. America is keen to buy British crime dramas.

Key Term

Spin-off
A new programme that is inspired by an existing one. Links to an existing programme make the new programme easier to market.

Task

Think of an idea for a spin-off for an existing crime drama. How will you market the new programme to an audience?

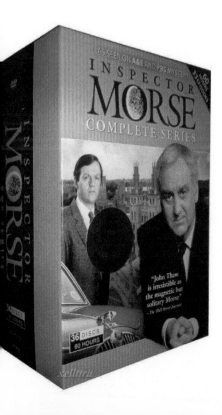

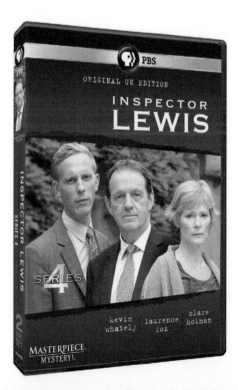

Media organisations

Scheduling guides

Each television channel employs schedulers and planners to decide which programme appears where in the daily schedule. Television scheduling strategies are used to give programmes the best possible chance of attracting and retaining an audience. They are used to give audiences programmes they are most likely to want to watch at the time they want to watch them. Schedules used to be a very important factor for audiences in planning their viewing; however, now viewing habits are changing and audiences watch programmes in different ways and at different times.

Television schedulers use a range of techniques to try to make sure that the audience stays with that channel and its programmes.

Look at the promotional description for a television drama designed to attract an audience to the programme, like this one for *Broadchurch*. What can you tell about the programme from the description and images used?

Key Terms

Prime time
This is the time when most people watch television and when the most popular programmes are scheduled. It is usually thought to be about 7–9.30pm, although the main family viewing time is 7–8pm.

The watershed
This is after 9pm and is the time when the channel's suggestion is that the programmes scheduled after this time will not be suitable for younger children. Individual channels have the responsibility for deciding which programmes appear before or after the watershed.

Why are schedules important to advertisers?

What is the impact of new technologies like BBC iPlayer on the schedules?

What effect will 'watch again' facilities have upon advertising for commercial television channels like ITV?

Task

Look at a copy of one week's television schedule and answer the following questions:

- Which television crime dramas are in **prime time**?
- Which television crime dramas are post **watershed**? Why do you think this is?
- Which are the popular sub-genres?
- Can you find an example of a hybrid genre?
- Can you find examples of the following scheduling techniques used for television crime drama:

  Zoning – this is where part of the schedule is devoted to a particular genre; for example, Channel 5 zones American crime dramas like *CSI: Miami*. The hope is that fans of the genre will stay with the channel to watch all the programmes in the 'zone'.

  Stripping – this is where a particular programme is scheduled at the same time every day, for example soap operas.

  Two-parters – this is where a television drama is scheduled over two nights, usually Sunday and Monday. This is to encourage the audience to watch that channel for both nights.

The importance of the ratings

Television channels are constantly in competition with each other for their audiences. The ratings regularly report which programmes have attracted the highest number of viewers. These are often reported in the national press, so audiences can see which are the popular channels and programmes. For the **commercial channels** like ITV, Channel 4 and 5, the ratings will help to attract advertisers to place adverts in the breaks in these programmes. For the BBC channels, the figures help to justify the licence fee, particularly at the moment when it is under a lot of criticism. For the programme producers the ratings are equally important – good figures will mean they can make another series, poor figures and the programme may disappear from our screens. Channels may take the decision to axe programmes if the ratings have fallen and they have to make cut-backs. Some programmes run as **pilot programmes** to assess the interest of an audience before a full series is made. BBC will often use BBC 2 as a test run for programmes to see how popular they are.

Key Terms

Commercial channels
These are the channels like ITV and Channel 4 who raise their money through advertising, unlike the BBC which gets its money from the licence fee.

Pilot programme
This is a one-off programme which is aired to see what the audience response will be. If the response is good then more programmes may be made.

Go to www.barb.co.uk, the official ratings website. BARB collates all of the viewing figures for all of the channels. From the information find out:

Task

- Which are the most popular television crime dramas on the main terrestrial channels? Why do you think this is?
- What are the most popular sub-genres? Why do you think this is?
- Do the viewing figures differ from channel to channel? Which are the most popular channels?

Key Figure

BARB
This stands for Broadcasters' Audience Research Board. BARB is owned by the BBC, ITV, Channel 4, Channel 5, and BSkyB. Its job is to provide audience figures and information for these channels.

How are new television crime dramas promoted?

It is important when a new television programme is launched that the audience are aware of it. All channels are in competition and their aim is to secure the audience for their programme. Audiences can be targeted in several different ways:

- Through the scheduling guides and listings magazines – some may include features introducing new series, the return of a programme or stars, like this example from *Radio Times*.
- Through articles and reviews in magazines and newspapers.
- Through interviews with the 'stars' of the programmes in the press and on talk shows and radio programmes.
- Through adverts on billboards and in magazines.

Key Terms

Series
This is a long-running television programme such as a hospital drama. Each episode of a series has a self-contained storyline and can be watched by a 'one-off' audience. However, it also contains storylines that link one episode to another.

Enigma
This is where the amount of information given to the audience is controlled in order to capture their interest and make them ask questions about the narrative, e.g. the shadow on the wall listening to the conversation.

Flagship programme
This is a programme that is important for the channel; this may be because it brings in high ratings, has a strong place in the schedule or is long running and therefore has a loyal audience.

Ident
This is a short visual image that appears between television programmes. It works as a logo to market the channel, for example the short films on BBC.

Tip

Producing storyboards and other practical tasks helps to prepare you for Section B of the examination paper.

● Through trailers on television. Trailers for a new drama **series** generally begin to appear on the screens two to three weeks before the programme is transmitted. They want to draw the audience's attention to the programme and to raise expectations. If the programme has a cast of recognisable 'stars' then the trailer will focus on them. If not, the focus may be on the narrative. The trailer will contain **enigmas** to make the audience want to watch the programme to find out what happens. Voice-overs give the audience an outline of the narrative, and music often adds to the overall effect. Even long-running series like *New Tricks* will produce trailers to remind audiences what to expect.

TASK   Look at a trailer for the crime drama *Scott & Bailey*: How does it attract audiences to watch the programme?

TASK   Design a double-page spread for a television listings magazine featuring a new crime drama.

Sometimes television channels will produce trailers focusing just on a specific genre, e.g. crime drama, to showcase their range of programmes. This is often done at certain times of the year, for example Christmas and autumn, or when the channel wants to celebrate their **flagship programmes** or a new crime series.

Practical task

Produce a storyboard for a trailer for one of the terrestrial channels for their crime drama programmes or for one specific programme. Use a scheduling guide to help you to look at the range of programmes produced by the channel in this genre, or research a particular programme. Remember to focus on crime dramas. Think about the techniques that are used:

● Edited highlights of action and drama.

● Close-ups of recognisable characters and stars.

● Appropriate music which the audience will come to associate with that particular programme.

● Clues to the narrative and enigmas to create interest.

● A voice-over to take the audience through the different clips. If the trailer is for a range of programmes, the voice-over will also promote the channel and the quality of the programmes on offer. If the trailer is for one programme, the voice-over will create drama and tension and give any additional information.

● Graphics sequences to reinforce the channel or programme branding, for example the BBC 2 **ident**.

Evaluate your storyboard, demonstrating how you would attract audiences to the channel and to the crime dramas.

Media texts

Credit and opening sequences

The title, **credit** and **opening sequences** of a television crime drama are important in letting the audience know the sub-genre of the programme and in raising their expectations of what they will see. This is very important for new dramas, but regular dramas will signal the start of the programme by a recognisable tune and a series of graphics or images that audiences will associate with the programme.

Key Terms

Credit sequence
This is usually the same every week and includes the name of the programme, the stars, the production company, etc. Sometimes this will appear at the start; sometimes it comes after some of the narrative has been introduced.

Opening sequence
This comes after the credit sequence and generally introduces the narrative and the main characters. It may include enigmas to hook the audience and keep them watching.

Task

Watch a selection of credit and opening sequences of television dramas. Answer the following questions:

- What information about the programme does the sequence give the audience?
- How do the graphics give information about the programme to come?
- How have music and other audio codes been used to give clues to the pace and the style of the programme that will follow?
- Which characters are introduced? What do you think their roles will be in the programme?
- How have the narrative or specific plot situations been introduced?
- What clues are given about the sub-genre? For example, is there iconography to suggest the sub-genre is forensics?
- What other codes and conventions of the genre/sub-genre/hybrid genre have been used in the sequence?

Practical task

Storyboard a new opening sequence for a television crime drama that you know well. Use your answers to the questions above to help you to decide what to include. Remember your aim is to attract and maintain your target audience.

Quickfire
24

What would you expect to see in an opening sequence for a new television crime drama?

Media texts: analysing crime dramas

Although crime dramas fall into different sub-genres, e.g. forensic, private detective, etc., they still share a repertoire of elements that places them in the crime drama genre. They can be a series or a **serial**.

Key conventions of crime dramas

Characters

Interesting main characters who may not always follow the rules, e.g. *Sherlock*, *Case Histories*.

Protagonists with personal problems and past histories which may come back to haunt them, e.g. *Luther*.

Often the main character doesn't get on with his bosses or with authority and feels he is not listened to, e.g. *Endeavour*.

There may be a one main detective, a pair or a team. Sidekicks are often different from the main detective – this provides interesting plot situations, e.g. *Lewis*.

Lewis and Hathaway, the detective pair in *Lewis*

Different sub-genres have different types of characters. For example, they may be a forensic officer, a private detective or a lawyer, for example *Silent Witness*.

Audiences become familiar with the main characters in crime dramas as they have been established over time. They can recognise them and know how they will behave.

The team in *Silent Witness*

TASK

Watch the trailers for *Luther*. How do you know that this is a character with problems?

Characters in crime dramas

Write a paragraph about each of these images of characters from crime dramas commenting on: iconography, clothing, mode of address, expression, gestures, etc. What clues are there to the sub-genres in which they appear?

TASK

TASK

Create profiles for three characters to appear in a new crime drama.

Explain how they will be represented:

- Their appearance.
- Their personality.
- Their role within the narrative.

Setting and iconography

- This is often established from the start and becomes recognisable to audiences. This may be a city setting or a village.

- Locations within the crime drama will often reflect the genre and will include recognisable iconography. This may be police stations, post mortem rooms and private houses.

- The setting may also say something about the main characters, for example Sherlock and Watson's rooms in *Sherlock*. The hi-tech police offices in *CSI: Miami* suggest state of the art police procedures.

- Iconography may include weapons, crime scene tape, plastic gloves, etc.

A scene from *Luther*

How does the setting of the crime drama give clues to the sub-genre and the possible storylines?

Think of three settings which would appear in your new crime drama. Explain them and how they will reflect the sub-genre and the narrative.

Technical and audio codes

- Dialogue may include the language used by police officers in their work. This may include particular words they use at a crime scene or when they arrest someone.

- Signature tunes and music used within the crime drama will give clues to the narrative and raise audience expectations.

- Some crime dramas experiment with interesting and unusual technical codes, *CSI: Miami* has high production values and uses slow motion, bird's eye view shots and flashback sequences; *Sherlock* uses CGI post-production effects to suggest what Sherlock is thinking as he tries to solve the crime.

- Lighting can suggest the narrative. The **lighting** in *Waking The Dead* is **low key** reflecting the 'dark' nature of the crimes they are investigating, whilst *CSI: Miami* uses **high key lighting** to suggest that the criminal cannot hide and the crime will be solved.

- Establishing shots are quick ways of showing the locations used in the crime drama, some of which will be recognisable to audiences.

Media texts: narrative

All media texts tell stories, both fact and fiction – these are called **narratives**. The producers of media texts use a variety of techniques to show the narrative to the audience.

Narrative structures

In television crime drama, as with other media texts, there are two types of narrative, **linear** and **non-linear**. Usually the audience is introduced to the hero/heroine and the world in which they live before that world is disrupted. Linear narrative was an idea discussed by the theorist Todorov; he decided that the narrative progressed through certain stages, one bit of action follows on from another.

In diagram form it would look like this:

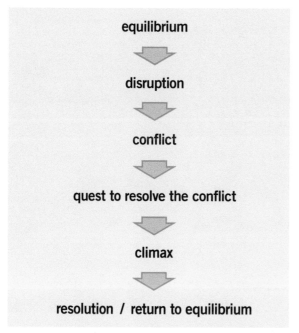

equilibrium

disruption

conflict

quest to resolve the conflict

climax

resolution / return to equilibrium

During the narrative the characters change as a result of what happens in the story and the **equilibrium** at the end may be very different from at the beginning.

Key Terms

Linear narrative
This is where the events in the story happen in order, one after another.

Non-linear
This is where the story moves around in time using techniques like flashbacks.

Equilibrium
This is the state of the story world at the beginning of the narrative where everything is stable.

Disruption
This is what changes that world; it may be a character or an event, for example a murder.

Key Figure

Todorov
A Russian theorist who explored the structure of stories.

Task

Using the diagram above, plot a narrative from a television crime drama you have seen recently. This can be the whole narrative or a sub-plot in an episode.

Now use the diagram to think up a new narrative from a crime drama.

A non-linear or circular narrative plays around with time and space and is more challenging for an audience as the narrative moves backwards and forwards. In crime dramas there may be flashbacks in the narrative to fill in gaps in the audience's knowledge or to explain why a character is behaving in a particular way. Often the drama starts with the crime and then moves back in time to show how and why the crime was committed.

Narrative techniques in crime dramas

The producers of crime dramas use a range of techniques to hold the interest of the audience. Most crime dramas are part of a series so it is important that the audience is left waiting for the next episode.

Split screen narratives. This technique is used in some television dramas. The screen is split into three or four sections with different narratives going on in each small screen.

Three strand narratives. This is a common narrative convention of regular television crime dramas. At the beginning of the programme three stories will be introduced, for example continuing tensions between colleagues, the investigation of a case that started in a previous episode and a case that is new for that particular episode. As the programme develops, the **narrative strands** cross over each other until the final conclusion. One of the strands may continue into the next episode and the others may finish in this episode. This will attract loyal and 'one-off' viewers.

A plot situation in *CSI*

Key Terms

Narrative strand
This is one storyline in the programme which may focus on one particular character or event and may run alongside other strands in the same programme.

Cliffhanger
This is where the audience are left with an enigma at the end. This encourages the audience to watch the next episode to find out what happened.

Look at the still image from *CSI*. Explain how this plot situation is one an audience would expect in a crime drama?

Tip

What you learn about narrative in television can be transferred to film texts you may study.

Sarah Lund and colleague in *The Killing*

Flexi-narrative. This is a more complex narrative structure with several storylines going on at the same time. This means the audience has to concentrate to understand what is happening and this keeps them watching. In these more complicated storylines there will be twists and turns and surprises.

A good example is the Danish crime drama *The Killing* where the audience are led along various narrative lines. At the end of each episode there is always a **cliffhanger** or a narrative twist which takes the audience by surprise and encourages them to watch the next episode.

Narrative codes in moving image texts

Flashbacks are used to give the audience additional information. They may also involve the audience with a character by seeing some of their past, which helps them to understand the narrative. They are also a way to manipulate time and space within the narrative. For example, *Life on Mars* and *Ashes to Ashes*, where most of the narrative takes place in the past.

Apparently impossible positions where the camera gives the audience a view of the action from an unusual position, for example in the air or from behind a wall. Audiences tend to accept this view if the narrative itself is believable as this makes them feel more involved. In crime dramas you may be watching the crime from above. This clearly makes the scene more tense.

Privileged spectator position – here the audience are shown parts of the narrative that other characters cannot see. For example, a close-up shot showing the audience a character taking a knife out of her pocket. The audience can then anticipate the action that will follow later in the narrative.

Point of view shots allow the audience to see the action from different perspectives. The camera may position the audience as the eyes of the murderer or the victim or may move between the two in order to build tension.

Enigma codes are used in both audio-visual and print texts. In television crime dramas the camera may only show some of the narrative, leaving the audience with unanswered questions. This is part of the appeal of a crime drama, as the audience will enjoy working out the clues and solving the crime along with the detectives.

Action codes are shorthand for moving the narrative along quickly. The packing of a suitcase means a journey; the placing of a gun in a bag suggests action will follow later in the story.

A voice-over is used to move the action on or to fill in missing information.

QuickFire 27

How do technical codes help to involve an audience in a crime drama?

Media texts: representation in television crime drama

What is meant by representation in crime dramas? In Section 2 you learned about the importance of representation as a media concept related to all media texts, here we are going to apply it specifically to crime drama.

In the context of Media Studies, representation means the way in which groups in society, including gender, age, ethnicity and national/local identity, are presented to an audience by different media texts. Television crime dramas are fictional texts but they show the audience a world that they are asked to believe in. However, this world is put together in a particular way to appear more exciting and dramatic in order to engage audiences to watch the programme. What do you think a day in the life of a real-life detective is like? How is it different from the television version?

Task

Plan a series of shots for a short extract from a new crime drama using some of the narrative codes suggested here. You can include the characters and settings that you planned in the earlier tasks in this section.

Key questions related to representation

What kind of world is represented by the media text? How do crime dramas try to show real life? Are British and American dramas different?

Calleigh and Horatio in *CSI: Miami*

How are stereotypes used in the text? What is their purpose?

Who is in control of the text? Are there any ideas and values shown in the representations, e.g. how different regions of Britain are presented in particular crime dramas like *Vera*?

Who is the target audience of the text? Will different audiences respond to the representations in different ways? Will women respond differently to the representations contained in *Scott & Bailey*?

What messages are contained within the text? What effect will the representations have upon the audience?

How are representations constructed in television crime dramas?

- Through technical codes – camera shots, angles and editing all contribute to the representations in the drama. For example, a low angle shot of a character in a drama can make them appear more intimidating. The camera can also position the audience to feel sorry for a character.

- The final editing will construct the representation for an audience. What we see finally is not real life; it has been edited to offer a version of reality. It will have been made more interesting to attract an audience.

- Through audio codes – sound will give clues to characters and their roles. Sinister music may start when a villain appears.

- Through the use of iconography. For example, what a character is wearing will send out messages as to whether they are a detective, a police officer, a victim or a villain.

Tip

For Section A of the examination paper you will need to study how social groups are represented in Television Crime Drama in terms of: **gender, ethnicity, cultural diversity, age and nation.**

You will need to use specific examples you have studied in class in order to answer these more demanding questions on the paper.

QuickFire 28

What are the differences between the worlds represented in British and American crime dramas?

Analyse these images of representation from television crime dramas

TASK

Vera ITV

Area of representation:

Technical codes:

Iconography:

Different audience responses:

Luther BBC

Area of representation:

Technical codes:

Iconography:

Different audience responses:

Scott & Bailey ITV

Area of representation:

Technical codes:

Iconography:

Different audience responses:

Audience and television crime drama

You will need to investigate the following with regard to audience when you are studying Television Crime Drama:

- Who is the target audience? How do you know?

- The ways in which media texts position audiences. This may be to involve the audience or to make them respond in some way.

- The ways in which different audiences and users respond to, use and interpret different texts.

55

Task

Apply the uses and gratifications theory to some of the examples of crime dramas you have investigated in class.

Tip
If there is an audience question in the examination, look for the key word to help you to answer it, for example target or appeal.

- The ways in which media texts target and appeal to audiences. All media industries are trying to make sure that they sell their products to an audience and are successful. Audiences are targeted through:

  – The language and mode of address used.

  – The way in which the programme is constructed.

  – Technical and audio codes.

- What affects the way in which an audience responds to a programme, e.g. their age, how they were brought up, their gender, etc?

Audience theories: uses and gratifications

This theory suggests that audiences 'use' different media texts for different reasons:

For entertainment and diversion – audiences watch or read some media texts in order to escape from everyday life. Audiences like to become involved in the solving of the crime along with the detectives.

For information and education – some texts are used by audiences when they want to know what is going on in other areas of society, for example in the world of the private detective.

For social interaction – some media texts are 'of the moment' and are discussed by the audience as they happen. This is sometimes referred to as **'water-cooler' television**. Audiences watch the programme so that they can then talk to others about it. An example would be when audiences went on social networking sites and tweeted after the last episode of *Sherlock* giving their opinions of what had happened. Here, the audience response was immediate and to be involved it is essential to keep up to date with the programme. This discussion continued up until Series 3 in January 2014 and was an effective way of keeping the programme in the minds of the audience.

Sherlock – Cross-platform responses

For personal identity – this is the idea that audiences will enjoy some media texts because they are able to compare their lives with the characters in them. The appeal of the programme may be that an audience can relate to a particular character in a situation and be involved with how they handle it.

TASK

Complete the following table :

Name of television crime drama	Entertainment/ diversion	Social Interaction	Personal identity	Information

Audience research

Ask a range of different audiences which television crime dramas they watch and why? What conclusions can you draw about why audiences watch crime dramas?

GCSE audio-visual Textual investigation: narrative

Explore how the narrative is constructed in (your chosen texts).

You must use the following to help you to plan your work:

- Discuss the **two main programmes** in your investigation. These should not be discussed equally, you can choose one programme to analyse in detail and then compare it with the second text, highlighting any similarities or differences. You will need to select relevant scenes.

- **You can present your work as a written essay.** You can use images/screen shots in your work, e.g. you can find an image from the programme and annotate it to show your understanding of narrative.

- **You can present your work as a PowerPoint presentation** incorporating annotated images, bullet pointed information, etc. If you choose this option you must ensure that you still demonstrate analytical skills and meet the word length.

Your work must be **400–850 words** in length.

Key Words

Try to use some of the words below in your investigation:
- Linear
- Non-linear
- Privileged spectator
- Apparently impossible positions.

Introduction

Explain what you understand by the term narrative in crime drama. Keep this general. Do not refer to the set texts yet. Discuss the structure of crime drama narratives. Here you could show your understanding of different structures, e.g. linear and non-linear. You may want to introduce the idea that British and American crime dramas are different and appeal to different audiences. Explain the texts you will use and which extracts you will be discussing.

Analysis

Now comment on the following in the two programmes remembering to focus on the construction of the narrative. Also consider how the audience will respond to this construction.

- **Characters** – are they conventional for this sub-genre or are they different? What is their role in the narrative? How do representations help the narrative? How may an audience respond to the characters? You can find an image from the programmes you have studied and annotate it to make your points clearer. Here is an example:

Vera could be said to be an unconventional detective.

She is an older more 'frumpy' woman as shown by her clothing which is sensible. She is not a power dresser. This suggests she may be a little eccentric.

She is pictured in an isolated rural setting which may gives clues to the narrative.

Her sidekick is male and much younger. Here he is pictured behind her suggesting she is more important. His clothing is more modern. Their differences may cause conflict in the narrative.

- **Setting and iconography** – how do we know we are watching a crime drama? How are the settings different in the two programmes? What is their role in the narrative? You can include an image and annotate it.

- **Technical and audio codes** – give examples from the programmes of any camera shots, angles, editing techniques, for example split-screen narrative, or any sounds that help to construct the narrative. Remember to include specific examples and shots that are specific to the narrative.

- **Narrative devices** – analyse any other devices/techniques used to construct the narrative, e.g. enigma codes, flashbacks. How conventional are these? What is the effect on audience?

Conclusion

Briefly sum up how you have answered the initial question.

Tip

Choosing texts that are contrasting will allow you to show your ability to explore different narratives. Remember one of the programmes will be your main text and the other will be used for comparison.

Tip

Remember that to gain marks in the higher levels you need to show your understanding of audiences and organisations in relation to this topic.

Tip

Information included in other sections of this book will help you with this investigation.

6: Advertising and Marketing

In 2015 the examination topic is Advertising and **Marketing**.

Section A will be Print Advertising

Section B will be Television Advertising

Advertising is an interesting and important media topic as it crosses all media platforms. Every media organisation needs to sell what it makes and so it advertises its products to its audience. This examination topic clearly links the three elements of the Media Studies Framework discussed earlier in this book – text, organisations and audience:

Genre: the codes and conventions of print and audio-visual advertisements.

Narrative: how advertisements are structured and how they tell stories in order to sell the product to an audience.

Representations: how advertisements use stereotypes, how they represent people, places, issues and events.

Organisations: how the producers of advertisements promote their products to audiences; how the industry is controlled and regulated.

Audiences/users: how audiences are targeted; the appeal of adverts; how audiences are categorised to make them easier to target.

The advertising industry is very big and very powerful, today more so than ever, as there are so many ways in which audiences can be targeted by advertisers.

Key Term

Marketing
This is the promoting and selling of products and services including advertising.

Tip

Look back at Section 2 Media Studies Framework to remind yourself of the important areas of this course. You can then bear them in mind when you are exploring this topic.

Task

Discuss the following statements about advertising. Think about which ones you agree with and which ones you don't. Try to not just say 'yes' or 'no', but support your opinions with specific examples.

- Advertisements persuade us to buy what we want, not what we need.
- Some advertisements are more interesting than the television programmes.
- Some advertisements cost as much to make as a short film.
- Advertisements can inform and educate us.
- Advertisements use stereotypes to transmit messages quickly.
- Advertisements can be misleading and don't always tell the whole truth.

Name five ways in which you may come across an advertisement in your normal day.

Who advertises and why?

We tend to think of advertising as being the selling of **consumable products** like shampoo, clothing and household products, but advertising is very broad and lots of organisations and people use advertising to communicate information. For example:

- Charities – to raise our awareness about an issue and to persuade us to donate money or help in some way.
- Government departments, for example Health – to give us information about health issues, for example healthy eating.
- Organisers of events, for example sporting competitions and pop concerts – to let us know they are happening and to persuade us to attend.
- The media – to promote new films and television programmes, for example.
- Schools, colleges and universities – to give information about courses and to persuade us to go there to study.
- Ordinary people – to sell items, find jobs or make announcements.

Where?

There are lots of ways in which advertisers of products and services can reach us including:

- Television and radio
- Cinema
- Mobile phones
- The Internet
- Sides of buses and bus shelters
- Billboards
- Magazines and newspapers
- Leaflets and flyers.

TASK

Find a specific example of an advert from each of the types listed here, for example a specific sporting event in your area.

Targeting a new audience

A successful advertisement catches our attention and makes us remember the product. Existing and new products both need to remind us that they exist. Products that have been around for many years, for example Cadbury's and Coca Cola, think up new ways to attract a new audience. Established **brands** are in competition with cheaper, supermarket brands and they have to persuade an audience to stay with them.

The aim of any advertisement is to target a wide audience. Companies switch agencies in order to bring new ideas to an advertising campaign and older brands have to 'reinvent' themselves regularly with new campaigns for new generations of consumers.

TASK

Think of some brands other than those already mentioned that have had to continue to attract audiences over a number of years.

What strategies have they introduced to do this, for example new packaging? Try to give specific examples.

Consider how you would market the following products to a new audience:

- Baby products to a male target audience
- A performance car to women
- Sportswear for an older audience
- Perfume to a male target audience
- Beer for women
- Coke for an older audience
- Healthy snacks to children
- Household cleaning products to men.

Choose one of the products above and its new audience. Give ideas for your marketing campaign including:

- Ideas for a slogan
- Images you would use
- Ideas for a TV advert including music, etc.
- Ideas for a magazine advert
- Other advertising strategies, e.g. celebrity endorsement.

What techniques do advertisers use to attract an audience?

Name – getting this right is very important. The name of a new product may suggest something about the product's image. Think about what the name Jaguar suggests about the car.

A slogan – is usually linked to something about the product and can be memorable. Sometimes they include a rhyme or suggest how the product may change your life.

TASK

1. Think of three existing names of products. What do they suggest about the product?

2. Think of three existing slogans. What techniques have they used to be memorable?

3. Think of a name and a slogan for the following **new products**:
   - A car
   - A fragrance
   - A toothpaste
   - A household cleaner.

   Briefly explain why you made the decisions you did and what the name and slogan suggest about the new product.

JUST DO IT.

Key Term

Unique selling point
Unique means different, so this phrase used by advertisers means the product has something about it that is different from other products and this will help to sell it.

Are there any disadvantages to celebrity endorsement?

Which adverts are more likely to use members of the public to endorse products?

Logo – this is the small design used on all promotional materials for a product. The audience will come to recognise it. In this Nike example, the logo and slogan are together. There is no clue to the actual products, but an audience recognise the brand and what it produces.

Endorsement – this is when advertisers use celebrities or ordinary members of the public to say how good the product is in the hope that this will persuade the audience to buy it. Everyday products like washing powders and DIY products tend to be endorsed by ordinary people as audiences are more likely to believe that they actually know about the product. Celebrity endorsers can attract an audience to the product quickly as they are easily recognised. They may have a link to the product, for example a glamorous celebrity would be more likely to endorse a more expensive brand, for example Keira Knightley and *Chanel.*

B&Q *Unloved Rooms* **campaign**

Unique selling point – this is the part of the product that makes it different from other similar products. This could be a 'new' ingredient for a food or a new feature of a mobile phone, for example.

Originality – the advertising industry is very competitive so some adverts entertain us rather than telling us very much about the product. 3's dancing pony was one of the most watched advertisements on YouTube in 2013. It was accompanied by the slogan 'Silly Stuff. It Matters.' Its quirkiness raised awareness of the brand.

3's dancing pony

Hard sell – this is 'in your face' advertising. Hard sell advertisements on television are usually short, loud and tell you the price. Sometimes they include a 'character' who gives you information. It is as if someone has come into the room to sell you the product personally.

Soft sell – this sort of advertising tends to sell a lifestyle or an image and the actual product is not always obvious until the end of the advert. These adverts are usually longer and have cost more to make.

Find some examples of hard sell and soft sell advertisements. What techniques do they use to attract audiences to their products?

Iconic representation – this is where the picture of the product appears in the advert. This is so that the audience know what to look for if they decide to buy. This technique is common in adverts for fragrances. In this advert for Tresor by Lancôme, the name of the product and the image of the bottle take up almost as much page space as the image of the product endorser.

Demonstrative action – this is where you see the product being used. This is often used to show you how easy something is to use, for example hair dye or straighteners.

Visual codes – the other aspects of the advert that we see are important, for example the use of colours, the gesture and expression of the people in the advert, the setting and iconography, etc.

Language – the spoken or written language is important in selling the product. Advertisements have to use persuasive language to sell the product. They will use **hyperbole** and will join words together to make the product seem interesting, for example 'taste-tempting'.

Mode of address – this is the way in which the text 'speaks' to the audience. This may be the fact that the person in the central image is looking straight at you or that in a television advert they are talking directly to you.

Technical codes – for both print and audio-visual advertisements you need to be aware of the types of shots and the editing used. For example, an advert for a romantic fragrance will use shots of a longer duration, and fades as part of the editing. An advert for a performance car may use fast-paced editing and close-up shots to show the car's features.

Audio codes – for audio-visual adverts sound is important. This may be the use of sound effects, for example the sound of the car's engine, the dialogue or the music used to go along with the images. Sometimes a memorable **jingle** will have been created specifically linked to the product. Sound in advertisements can be both **diegetic** and **non-diegetic**.

TASK

QUICKFIRE 32

How would you recognise a hard sell print advert?

Key Terms

Hyperbole
This is over-exaggerated language used to make the product seem better than it is.

Jingle
This is a catchy little song that focuses on the product. Jingles are important for radio adverts as you can't see the product and what it does.

Diegetic sound
This is 'sound you can see'. That is sound that is visible in the frame and is part of the action, for example the crunch of the crisp being eaten.

Non-diegetic sound
This is sound that is off screen, for example the use of a pop song as a soundtrack for a fragrance advert.

Tip
Paying attention to the length of the advertisement will give you a clue to how much it cost to make.

Internet advertising

This is quite a recent form of advertising. Many **advertising agencies** use this platform as modern audiences are less likely to catch the adverts on the television and a wide range of different audiences use the Internet at all times of the day and night.

The techniques used in Internet advertising are a bit different from other forms:

Web banners – these appear on the page of the website you are using, for example your email account. They usually feature an image and are on horizontal or vertical boxes. If you click on them they take you to the advertiser's website.

Pop ups – these are adverts that 'pop up' when you are using the web page. They are often used to capture email addresses so that the advertiser can then target the user directly. Often they encourage you to 'click' by offering a chance to win something.

Pop unders – these are the adverts that appear when you shut down the web page.

Email marketing – this is where you get an email advert sent directly to your in-box. This could be for a company or a shop you have bought something from in the past who want to encourage you to shop with them again. They may tempt you by special offers.

Contextual advertising – these are adverts that are linked to Internet searches you have done. For example, if you have been searching to buy a pair of trainers, adverts for these products will begin to appear when you use the Internet.

Search engine marketing – this is where companies will pay to appear at the top of the list of a search. This means they are more visible to the user and they may be more likely to click on them first.

Key Term

Advertising agencies
Most makers of products do not make the adverts for the products themselves. They will use an advertising agency whose job it is to research the target audience and then create a campaign to sell the product.

QUICKFIRE 33

Why do some adverts choose to use memorable pop songs?

QUICKFIRE 34

What are the advantages of the Internet for advertisers?

TASK

Monitor the different types of Internet advertising you come across in a week. Think about how much of it relates directly to you and your search habits and how much of it is random.

Audiences

It is important that advertising agencies know as much as possible about the target audience for their product. In advertising, it is particularly important to know how much money the audience may have to spend on the product. To help with this the industry categorises audiences in two main ways:

Demographic profile – this method groups audiences from group A to E according to their jobs and how much they earn. Group A are the wealthiest people and Group E have less money to spend on luxuries and include students, people on only the state pension and the unemployed.

Psychometric – this method groups audiences according to how people live their lives and what is important to them, their values. This method was thought up by Young and Rubicam, an advertising agency. The groups they came up with included:

- Mainstreamers: these are people who like security. They like to think they are getting value for money but they also like tried and tested brands.

- Aspirers: these are people who like designer labels. They want what they buy and wear to suggest something about them. They are persuaded by celebrity endorsement and are happy to pay for something they really want on credit.

Aspirers keep up-to-date with trends

Which group would this person fit into?

- Explorers: these are people who like to discover new things. They are attracted by brands that offer something new and different.

- Succeeders: these are people who feel they have nothing to prove so are not so interested in designer labels. They feel they deserve the best and will buy brands that are serious and reliable.

- Reformers: these are people who are not impressed at all by designer labels or fancy cars. They are concerned about the environment and living a healthy life.

Which one of the Young and Rubicam audience groups do you fit into and why?

Tip

The audience models discussed here are useful for explaining the appeal of adverts. However, they cannot be applied to all media texts.

For each of the above groups give examples of specific products you think they would be more likely to buy. For example, succeeders may buy a BMW car every time as it is a top of the range model but is also reliable.

Task

Quickfire 35

Why do you think Young and Rubicam's model of audiences may be more useful for advertisers?

Analysing a print advertisement

Now you need to try to put everything you have learned in this section together to help you to analyse examples of advertisements. Think about how this Olay advert featuring Olympic gold medal winner Jessica Ennis-Hill appeals to audiences.

Key Terms

Aspirational
This type of advertising makes the audience want to buy the product even though what it is selling, for example natural beauty and sporting achievement, may be out of their reach.

Brand identity
This means the meanings an audience will attach to a particular brand. This will be built up over time. The brand identity of Olay is that it is a reliable and inexpensive product for moisturising skin.

Tip

In an examination question for Section A you will be expected to show your ability to pick out and analyse key features of the text. You will also be expected to use media terminology in your answers.

The choice of celebrity endorser is interesting. She is not a glamour model, but someone who has achieved in sport.

The shot is a medium close-up shot and her face takes up most of the page. **Technical codes** of lighting have been used but she is not overly airbrushed, suggesting a more realistic **representation**. The soft colours add to this natural representation.

Her **mode of address** is direct and her expression suggests confidence. This is supported by the **anchorage** 'pushing the limits of what's possible'. She is an **aspirational** figure and women will look up to her. Further anchorage about the product emphasises that Olay products help to 'enhance her skin's natural beauty'. The product avoids making unrealistic claims.

One of the **visual codes** is her clothing. She is wearing a running vest reminding the audience of who she is and what she does. However, she is also wearing some make up and diamond earrings suggesting that she also likes beautiful things and to look attractive.

There is **iconic representation** of the product so that the audience know what it looks like; the **font style** used for the name of the product is also part of the **brand identity**.

Task

Find an example of a print advertisement. Investigate the techniques it has used to appeal to an audience. Remember to use media terminology.

Analysing a campaign: IRN-BRU

IRN-BRU is a product and a brand that has been around for a long time and has come up against competition from other soft drinks. The company has had to create a new **campaign** and a new image in order to re-launch itself and attract a new audience. It launched a cross-media campaign in 2012 with a new slogan: IRN-BRU: Gets You Through. The aim was to celebrate the Scots' ability to see the positive in difficult and embarrassing situations.

Key Term

Campaign
This is run by an advertising agency, in the case of IRN-BRU, Leith Agency. A campaign is a sequence of advertisements for a product and links the packaging, radio, TV, print and Internet adverts.

Text

The **genre** is soft drinks advertising. The aim of the campaign is to persuade the audience to buy an established brand rather than the supermarket one. The adverts in the campaign each have a short, funny, linear **narrative** involving a potentially difficult family situation. The problem or disruption is introduced in the beginning, for example in the first advert, *Steamy Windows*, a young boy comes home to catch his mum in an embarrassing situation, in another a young woman brings her new English boyfriend home to meet her very Scottish father! In each of the adverts the situation is made better when the person takes a drink from the can of IRN-BRU. Within the narrative structure, this is the attempt to resolve the problem.

IRN-BRU *New Fella* advertisement

In *Mum*, one of the most recent adverts (2013) in the campaign, a teenager arrives home with his friends where his mum discusses her new push up bra. The boy's embarrassment is reduced every time he takes a drink from the can and the situation seems better. The drink is not glamorised in the narrative it is just seen to restore the equilibrium and the ending is a happy one.

There are a range of **representations** constructed in the campaign including national identity. In fact the *New Fella* advertisement was said by some audiences to be anti-English in the way it represents the reactions of the father to the English boyfriend. Other representations seen in the campaign include teenagers and gender. The representation of teenagers is more realistic than in some advertisements, they are seen to be relatively 'ordinary', they are part of a family and are embarrassed by their parents.

IRN-BRU *Mum* advertisement

67

Organisations

Advertisements themselves need to be promoted just as they will be used to promote other products. The advertising agency responsible for the IRN-BRU campaign used a range of strategies to make sure these new adverts were seen. Agencies who are trying to target young people will often start with the platform most popular with them – the Internet and mobile phone technology. For the *IRN-BRU Baby* advert they used these stages of marketing, the most important being **word of mouth** marketing:

1st stage – the YouTube link tweeted by a single, solitary fan of the brand.

2nd stage – 100,000 views in 24 hours thanks to some co-ordinated **influencer** activity.

3rd stage – 650,000 views over 3 weeks as a result of spreading the word across different platforms.

4th stage – the television launch of the advert.

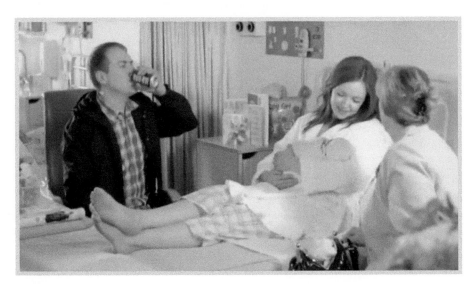

In less than a month there were over a million views and the link continued to be shared across Twitter. Three weeks after the initial tweet, the ad was aired in a few high profile television spots during the European Football Championship. This generated an additional 300,000 YouTube views in 48 hours and triggered hundreds of additional mentions of the link on Twitter.

Regulation

The advertising industry is regulated by the ASA, the Advertising Standards Authority. Its aim is to ensure that no one is offended by an advert, that they are shown at the appropriate time and that they are 'legal, honest, decent and truthful'. Ordinary members of the public can complain about an advert and the ASA must investigate the complaint. Indeed, several complaints were made about both the *IRN-BRU Baby* advert and the *Mum* advert.

QUICKFIRE 36

How is national identity represented in the *New Fella* advert?

QUICKFIRE 37

Why do you think the television advert was the last stage of this campaign?

Audience/users

Another key element of the IRN-BRU campaign is its website. Here **users** can view the campaign but also engage with the product in a range of other ways that make the brand memorable. This form of advertising has become more popular recently, particularly with a younger audience who spend less time watching television and more time on the Internet. The IRN-BRU site is very interactive and encourages the audience to become involved in promoting the product.

IRN-BRU website

Explore the website for IRN-BRU http://www.irn-bru.co.uk. Here you can also view the audio-visual and print advertisements for the whole campaign.

What activities and opportunities are available to the user?

Who is the audience for this product and how have they been targeted by the advertisements?

How does the website help to promote the product?

Note

Permission to use imagery for this case-study was sought by the publisher. IRN-BRU do not target their advertising or marketing at schools or schoolchildren. Schools and Colleges are responsible for overseeing their students' choice of advertising campaigns to analyse.

Key Term

User
This is another word for a type of audience. It suggests that the audience is asked to be active and to 'use' the text in some way. This is usually the case with websites where an audience can watch videos, send in responses and make choices when navigating around the site.

Task

How is the experience of a user of a website different from an audience that watches the advert on television?

Independent research

Visit the ASA website: www.asa.org.uk and investigate the complaints made about the IRN-BRU adverts and the decisions made by the ASA.

GCSE Practice Assignment

Section B : Thinking About the Media – Planning

This assignment will help to prepare you for the organisation and skills needed for your final production assignment.

Create a marketing campaign for a new product, for example a soft drink.

Research options

Print and audio-visual advertisements similar to the one you want to produce.

Websites for products similar to the one you want to produce.

Advertising agencies and their strategies.

Audiences and what they want from a new product.

Planning options

Produce a mock-up of a print advertisement for your product.

Produce a storyboard for a television advert for your product.

Produce the designs for a website promoting your product.

Ideas for the marketing and distribution of your campaign including packaging, logos, etc.

Production options

Produce two print advertisements for your new product.

Produce a short television advertisement for your product.

Design the home page and two other pages of the website for your product.

Evaluation

Explain how your production (where appropriate):

- Met your aims
- Used the codes and conventions of advertisements across different platforms
- Used representations
- Constructed a narrative
- Attracted and appealed to an audience
- Used effective marketing strategies.

QuickFire 39

Why is it important to find out the ideas and opinions of an audience in the early stages of your planning?

Tip

Practising skills like those in this assignment will help you to prepare for your final production piece.

Tip

For the higher marks, try to be a little bit original and not just copy an existing campaign.

GCSE Print Textual investigation: Representation of gender or age

Explore how gender or age are represented in (your 2/3 chosen texts).

You must:

- Discuss 2/3 print advertisements. One should be explored in more detail than the others.

- You can use images in your work; for example, you can find an image and annotate it to show your understanding of representation.

- Focus on how gender or age is represented in the examples.

- Your work must be 400–850 words in length.

- You can present your work as a PowerPoint presentation or as an **illustrated essay**.

Use the following to help you to plan your work.

Introduction

Explain what you understand by representation. Try to use some key words.

Explain generally how and why different advertisements may represent gender/age differently.

Main focus

Now investigate your chosen key advertisement exploring how gender or age is represented. You need to cover:

- **Visual codes**
  - Layout and design
  - Use of colour
  - Font choice and style
  - Clothing, setting, expression, gesture and technique.

- **Technical codes**
  - Camera shots – how does this add to the representation?
  - Camera angle – a low angle shot may make the main person in the advert seem more intimidating.
  - Post-production editing, for example, air brushing – what effect will this have on the representation?

- **Language and mode of address**
  - How do the words chosen and the mode of address contribute to the representation?
  - How is the language used to persuade an audience to buy the product?

- **Audience**
  - How does the way in which gender/age is represented affect the way in which an audience respond?

- **Organisation** – try to refer to regulation or how advertising agencies work.

Key Term

Illustrated essay
Here you can include images in the middle of your writing as evidence of the points you are making.

Key Words

Try to use some of the words below in your investigation.
- Construction
- Stereotype
- Context
- Anchorage
- Mediation.

Tip

Information included in other sections of this book will help you with this investigation.

Tip

Choosing print adverts that show different representations will allow you to show your ability to explore different representations.

71

Texts 2 and 3

Now use the headings above to explore your other advertisements. Try to choose examples that allow you to explore different representations of gender or age. For example, one of your texts may be one that is constructed to show an unrealistic, aspirational representation of a woman; another example may show a more realistic one, for example a mum.

Conclusion

This is an investigation so in your conclusion you need to briefly sum up what you have found out. This may include the following:

- Gender and age are represented differently according to the advertisement in which they feature.
- The way in which the representation is constructed may affect what the audience think of the product.
- Advertisements tend to use easily recognisable stereotypes of people to send out messages quickly.

Remember to make links to the specific advertisements you have explored in your investigation.

Success criteria

Lower Level 3

- You have explored the way in which gender/age is represented in your chosen texts in some detail.
- You have shown some awareness of the fact that the representation can have an effect on an audience.
- You have referred to more than one text.
- You have used some media vocabulary in your investigation.
- You have organised your investigation and shown your understanding of representation.

Lower Level 4

- You have shown an excellent ability to analyse the representations in your chosen advertisements. You have written about your texts in detail.
- You have shown an awareness of both the audience and the organisations that produce the text.
- You have confidently used a wide range of media terms in your investigation.
- You have shown that you clearly understand representation.
- Your writing and presentation are coherent and very accurate.

Key Term

Success criteria
These are the main things you need to include in your work so that you know that you have succeeded.

Tip

Always remember to include a conclusion. This, along with an introduction, gives your work a structure. It also allows you to demonstrate what you have found out.

Tip

Make sure that you choose texts that allow you to write a lot about them. Some advertisements have very little content and may be harder to explore.

7: Lifestyle and Celebrity

In this country over the past few years a '**celebrity culture**' has been established. We, as a media audience, have become very interested in the public and private lives of a whole range of celebrities from different areas of the media. The advances in technology, for example Twitter and other social networking sites, have made it easy to find out information about the lives of celebrities. This generation of young people, more than any other, feel that they can have a close relationship with someone who is a celebrity. As Media students you need to consider if this is a good or a bad thing.

Key Term

Celebrity culture
Celebrity culture is one where people are obsessed with famous people. These celebrities may not have actually accomplished much, but they often have extensive media coverage.

Task

Discuss and answer these questions in as much detail as possible:

- What do you understand by the term 'celebrity'? Write a definition of this term.
- Where, in the media, would you expect to find celebrities?
- Who would you say are the celebrities most in the media at the moment? Why do you think this is? What have they done?
- Are all celebrities represented in a positive way in the media? Give examples of media texts where you may get positive and negative representations of celebrities.
- Consider the following statements about stars and celebrities. What do you think?
    - 'Famous people need the media.'
    - 'The media should not invade the private lives of stars and celebrities.'
    - 'Stars are complex representations of real people.'

Independent research

Find out as much as you can about the phone-hacking scandal of 2013 and why it ended in the closing of *The News of The World*, a national Sunday paper and how this led to greater regulation of the press.

Task

Imagine that you work for the company that produces *I'm A Celebrity, Get Me Out Of Here.* You have been given an unlimited budget to persuade ten celebrities to take part in the programme. Who would you choose to appear on the next series of the programme?

For each celebrity you choose, give at least two reasons why they should be included.

Key Term

Endorse
If celebrities endorse a product they say that they use it and they think it is good. In this way the advertisers hope to persuade the audience, if they like the celebrity, to buy the product.

Celebrities and media organisations

Without the media, celebrities would not exist. Media texts are the ways through which stars and celebrities are marketed to an audience. Stars learn how to use certain media texts to their advantage, but they are not in control of some of the images that may appear in the media. Media texts, for example magazines, will be very aware of which celebrities are favoured by their readers and will feature them on the front covers or in the pages of the magazine. As many of us do not have direct access to our favourite stars, we rely on the media to give us information about them.

- How might the media affect an audience's response to a celebrity? For example, by the way in which photographs are used.

- How can celebrities ensure that they stay in the public eye?

- Why might advertisers want to use celebrities to **endorse** their products? Give some examples of celebrities who appear in advertisements for products. What are the advantages and disadvantages of this advertising technique?

Why do you think L'Oreal chose Cheryl Cole as their celebrity endorser?

Can you think of any disadvantages to using a celebrity to endorse a product?

Task

Think of an idea for a new product. Choose a celebrity you would use to endorse your product.

Consider:

- What your new product is, for example a fragrance.
- The name of your new product.
- Your choice of celebrity.
- Explain why you have chosen that celebrity.
- Mock up the print advertisement showing how your choice of celebrity would help to appeal to your audience.
- Annotate your design showing the decisions you have made.

Text: the representation of stars and celebrities in the media

Depending on the media text, stars and celebrities will be represented in different ways. Representation is an important media term and it means the way in which media texts, for example magazines, newspapers and television programmes, present people, events and issues.

The ways in which stars and celebrities are presented by different media texts will affect how the audience views and judges them. For example, the way in which magazines represent celebrities through their use of images, headlines and captions can have an effect on what the audience think about them.

When exploring how a particular star/celebrity is represented in a media text you will need to think about:

The way in which the media text is constructed:

● How have technical codes like camera shots and editing been used to construct the text?

● Does the **construction** give a positive or negative representation of the celebrity?

The way in which the anchorage contributes to the representation:

● How do the captions, headlines, language and mode of address used in the text contribute to the representation of the celebrity?

What ideas and messages are contained within the media text?

● What does the text want the audience to think about the celebrity? How do you know this?

How will different audiences respond to the representation of the celebrity?

● What will affect that response?

Key Terms

Construction
The way in which the text is put together, for example the choice of font, headline or main image.

Anchorage
The words that go with the image. They give the image meaning.

QUICKFIRE 42

Give a specific example of how a magazine may represent a celebrity.

Discuss how the images, construction and language are used to represent the celebrities on these newspaper front pages.

TASK

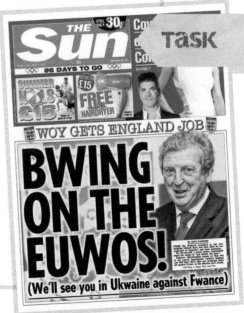

We have learned that how a celebrity is represented depends on the text in which they appear and the target audience. Below is a magazine featuring Kristen Stewart, in other parts of this section you will see how other texts represent this star in different ways in order to appeal to their audience. Think about how she is constructed here:

Norman Jean Roy / GQ © The Condé Nast Publications Ltd.

THE WORLD'S LEADING MEN'S MAGAZINE

BRITISH **GQ**

GENTLEMEN'S QUARTERLY

Man up!

Tony Parsons and Victoria Coren on the **new rules of masculinity!**

BITE ME!

Twilight's Kristen Stewart is ready to draw blood

By Jonathan Heaf

– Kristen Stewart photographed for British GQ by Norman Jean Roy

Phone hacking: Rupert Murdoch's secret vendetta

By Michael Wolff

GQ is a monthly men's magazine. It focuses on fashion, style and culture for men.

GQ stands for Gentleman's Quarterly; this suggests that the magazine is sophisticated and aimed at slightly older men with money who will be attracted by the lifestyle the magazine offers.

Although Kristen Stewart is represented here in quite a sexual way, she is also seen to be sophisticated through her code of clothing which is a retro bikini and is less revealing.

She is constructed for a male audience and so is represented as men would like to see her.

Her mode of address is direct; she is looking at the reader, they feel linked to her.

The camera shot used is a long shot to establish where she is, which gives a sense of luxury as she is on a sun lounger by a pool. The camera angle is high, making her appear vulnerable.

The visual codes also suggest the vampire link with her fame in the *Twilight* films. This is shown through the white skin, black clothing, black nail varnish and red lips. The anchorage of the cover line adds to this representation by saying she is 'ready to draw blood'. 'Bite me!' is an imperative and an invitation to the male reader who may find her representation appealing.

Quickfire 43

How has the representation of Kristen Stewart been constructed to suit the genre of magazine and the target audience?

Task

Design the front cover of either a film magazine or a women's magazine showing a different representation of Kristen Stewart. Annotate your design showing the decisions you have made in constructing her representation.

Audiences: Richard Dyer's Star theory

It is important, in studying any media topic, to explore the relationship between the media text and the audience. To help to develop your analysis of stars you can refer to theories and theorists. Richard Dyer studied a range of stars and celebrities to investigate what makes a star and how they appeal to audiences. His theory can be applied to a range of media texts. He discovered:

- A true star has a lasting importance and is a 'brand' that will stand the test of time.
- Stars have an identity or **persona** that goes beyond what they are associated with, for example making films.
- Stars are easily recognisable and their star image is recognisable and has meaning for audiences – this is why many stars are used in advertisements.

Stars as constructions

- Stars are constructed, artificial images. They often have a USP (unique selling point) that makes them easily recognisable to an audience, for example Beckham's tattoos, Jedward's hair. Fans of the star may copy the style of their favourite celebrity.

- Sometimes stars will change their image to keep the interest of their audience, for example Lady Gaga. They will reinvent themselves so that audiences do not become bored. Some stars have managed to stay in the public eye for many years.

- Stars are constructed by the media industry that creates them. Dyer said:
  'A star is an image not a real person that is constructed (as any other aspect of fiction is) out of a range of materials (e.g. advertising, magazines, etc., as well as films [music]).'

Industry and audience

- Stars are often manufactured to make money for the industry. The *X Factor* produces stars that they think the audience want. Where the industry finds a **formula** that works they will make more of the same.

- Artists are basically a product that needs to be sold in order to make profit just like any other business does.

- However, some audiences want stars that are a bit different. For example, the rise of the indie music genre that produces bands and artists that are less **mainstream**.

Give an example of a star/s that has been constructed to appeal to a specific audience.

Ideology and culture

Some stars have certain cultural values and attitudes – audiences may share these beliefs and therefore feel closer to the star – for example, the wearing of purity rings by The Jonas Brothers, and Cristiano Ronaldo who does not have tattoos so that he can give blood.

- A star may initiate a fashion trend/hairstyle/clothing that can be copied by fans, for example Marilyn Manson.

- We are a 'celebrity culture' – this is evident by the fact that there are several forms of media dedicated to celebrity gossip where fans can catch up with the lives of their favourite stars. Lady Gaga's website Littlemonsters.com works to build a community amongst fans who are dedicated to the star. She also uses this platform to give advice and support to her followers:
  'Be brave. Dare to create and share your art with the world. Be kind. Encourage and support your fellow monsters. We don't want to put anyone down, be it other Little Monsters or other artists.
  Be tolerant. Never make anyone feel unwelcome or judged; treat everyone with respect, love and acceptance.' (www.littlemonsters.com)

- Social networking sites and Twitter allow the star to develop their persona and to establish a following. Some people become obsessed by a star and their lives. Twitter, etc., has made stars more accessible. The rise in popularity of gossip magazines, for example *heat* and *Closer*, are further examples of media platforms which tap into the obsession with celebrity.

- Fans feel they have something in common with the stars and their **cultural values** because they know so much about them. However, it is often the case that we know very little about the actual star, only about the persona and character that the star and their producers have created.

What do you think is the formula for making a successful boy band?

Key Term

Cultural values
This is the idea of what is important or unimportant, right or wrong and is shared by a group of people.

> **TASK**
>
> Think of some other examples of stars who fit into the different sections of Dyer's theory.

Character and personality

QUICKFIRE 46

Why are social networking sites important to celebrities?

- Stars are presented as 'real' human beings. Although they are constructed, they have some aspect of reality which allows us to engage with them.

- Stars are a reflection of their time/generation – they can be glorified versions of 'us' and so we feel linked to them in some way.

- When we see a star's life in magazines we feel closer to them.

- Stars may use a media text, for example a CD cover, to present an image of themselves to the audience. They have control over how they are represented, which is not available to them in other media forms, for example gossip magazines.

- When stars play roles, their characters and personalities are created for them by someone else, e.g. the director of the film. It is sometimes the case that the audience cannot distinguish between the role played by the star and their real personality. This is particularly true where a star has played the same role for a long time, for example characters in soap operas.

Explore how different media texts represent the same star/celebrity in different ways

TASK

Study the way in which Kristen Stewart is represented across a range of different media texts. Comment on how the representation is constructed:

- The image used.
- The use of colour.
- The language and mode of address that anchors the image – what does this tell us about her? How are we encouraged to view her?
- Who is the target audience of the text? How does this affect the way in which the star is represented?
- Is the representation of this star positive or negative? How do we know?
- How will different audiences respond to the representation?

QUICKFIRE 47

Give an example of a media text where the star is in control of their image.

TASK

Choose a star/celebrity. Find examples of different media texts that represent that star, e.g.:

- Newspapers.
- Magazines – look at different genres.
- CD covers.
- Film posters.

Annotate your examples showing how they are represented. Think about:

- How the media text is constructed.
- Who is in control of the representation.
- How an audience may respond differently according to the text.

GCSE Thinking about the Media: Planning

Practice assignment: marketing a celebrity

Task

Take digital photographs of your friend/someone in your class and then make them into a celebrity!

Possible media texts to use for promotion of your celebrity:

- A CD cover
- A film poster
- A magazine interview/article
- A newspaper interview/report
- An advertisement
- A fashion promotion.

Research

Look at some existing examples of the above and consider how celebrities are promoted.

Planning – things to consider

- Composition of photographs – how are you/your partner going to look like a celebrity? Where are you going to take your photographs? You may need to do a recce.
- Shot types / angle
- Design and layout
- Use of colour
- Who are the target audience and how are they attracted?
- Text and language.

Production

Create your text using your own photography. Consider how you will construct your 'celebrity'.

Evaluation

When your product is finished you will need to write an evaluation discussing how your production:

- Met its aims and purpose
- Used appropriate generic conventions
- Used representations
- Used narrative (where appropriate)
- Addressed the audience
- Revealed media organisational issues.

Research evidence

- Annotated examples of similar texts.
- Ideas for fonts, colours, etc.
- Mood boards.
- Audience research: questionnaires/focus groups.

Planning evidence

- A log to show what needs to be done when.
- Photographs of recces.
- A range of different photographs of your celebrity.
- A mock-up of your text.

GCSE Print Textual investigation: representation of an issue

Explore how your chosen celebrity is represented in (your 2/3 chosen texts).

You must:

- Discuss 2/3 print media texts, for example CD covers, magazine pages and film posters. One should be explored in more detail than the others.
- You can use images in your work, for example you can find an image and annotate it to show your understanding of representation.
- Focus on how the celebrity is represented.
- Your work must be 400–850 words in length.
- You can present your work as a PowerPoint presentation or as an **illustrated essay**.

Use the following to help you to plan your work.

Introduction

Explain what you understand by representation. Try to use some key words. Look back at pages 20–21 to help you.

Explain generally how and why different media texts may represent celebrities differently.

Main focus

Now investigate your chosen key texts exploring how your chosen celebrity is represented in them. You need to cover:

Visual codes

- Layout and design
- Use of colour
- Font choice and style
- Clothing, expression, gesture and technique.

Technical codes

- Camera shots – how does this add to the representation?
- Camera angle – a low angle shot may make the star seem more intimidating.
- Post-production editing, for example airbrushing.

Language

- How do the words chosen and the mode of address contribute to the representation of the star?
- What clues does the language used give to the genre of the text?

Audience

How does the way in which the celebrity is represented affect the way in which an audience may view them?

Key Term

Illustrated essay
Here you can include images in the middle of your writing as evidence of the points you are making.

Tip

Information included in other sections of this book will help you with this investigation.

Tip

Choosing texts that are contrasting will allow you to use your ability to explore different representations.

Key Words

Try to use some of the words below in your investigation.
- Construction
- Stereotype
- Context
- Anchorage
- Mediation.

Tip

To attain the higher levels, consider how the organisation that produces the text may affect how your chosen celebrity is represented.

Texts 2 and 3

Now use the headings above to explore your secondary texts. Try to choose texts that allow you to explore different representations of celebrity. For example, one of your texts may be one where the celebrity is largely in control, like *Hello* magazine, and another may be *heat* magazine where the celebrity has limited control of how they are represented.

Conclusion

This is an investigation so in your conclusion you need to briefly sum up what you have found. This may include the following:

- Celebrities are represented differently according to the media text in which they feature.
- The way in which the celebrity is constructed may affect what the audience think of that star.
- Some texts have a lot of control over the way in which they represent the celebrity.

Remember to make links to the specific texts you have explored in your investigation.

Success criteria

Lower Level 3

- You have explored the way in which the celebrity is represented in your chosen texts in some detail.
- You have shown some awareness of the fact that the representation can have an effect on an audience.
- You have referred to more than one text.
- You have used some media vocabulary in your investigation.
- You have organised your investigation and shown your understanding of representation.

Lower Level 4

- You have shown an excellent ability to analyse the representations in your chosen texts. You have written about your texts in detail.
- You have shown an awareness of both the audience and the organisations that produce the text.
- You have confidently used a wide range of media terms in your investigation.
- You have shown that you clearly understand representation.
- Your writing and presentation are coherent and very accurate.

8: Vampire/Horror Genre

Audiences have been fascinated by vampires for many years and films have been made on this topic since *Nosferatu* in 1922 – the first film made featuring a vampire. Dracula as a character first appeared in a novel by Bram Stoker in 1897 and since then this character and other vampires have reappeared regularly in films and television programmes. In this section we are going to explore the popularity of the topic and also investigate how the storylines and characters have changed to attract more modern audiences whilst still keeping some of the key conventions of this genre.

This topic also allows you to explore how the genre is presented across a range of **media forms** including print, film and television.

How much do we know about vampires?

TASK

Write down as many points as you can about vampires, for example they don't like garlic.

Now discuss how you know this information.

TASK

Look at the images of vampires on page 84 taken from a range of forms including graphic novels, books and film stills.

- What can you say about the visual codes:
  - Facial expressions?
  - Clothing?
  - Gestures?
  - Use of colour?
- From these images what would you say were the typical features of a vampire?
- What are the similarities between the images?
- Are there any images that are different in any way? What are those differences?
- What do the technical codes, for example lighting, add to the representation?

TASK

Create a profile for a vampire that would appear in a new book, film or television programme. Use the following headings to help you: appearance, clothing, voice, likes and dislikes, habitat, recognisable features, name.

Key Term

Media form
This is the range of different ways the media can communicate with an audience, for example television, film, radio, etc.

Key Figures

Nosferatu
This was the name of the vampire in the film of the same name. Nosferatu was one of the earliest representations of a vampire in film. The film was released in 1922. It was a silent film and was based on the book *Dracula* by Bram Stoker.

Bram Stoker
He was the author of the 1897 Gothic horror novel *Dracula*. This novel first introduced the idea of the vampire we recognise now as Dracula.

Text: images of vampires

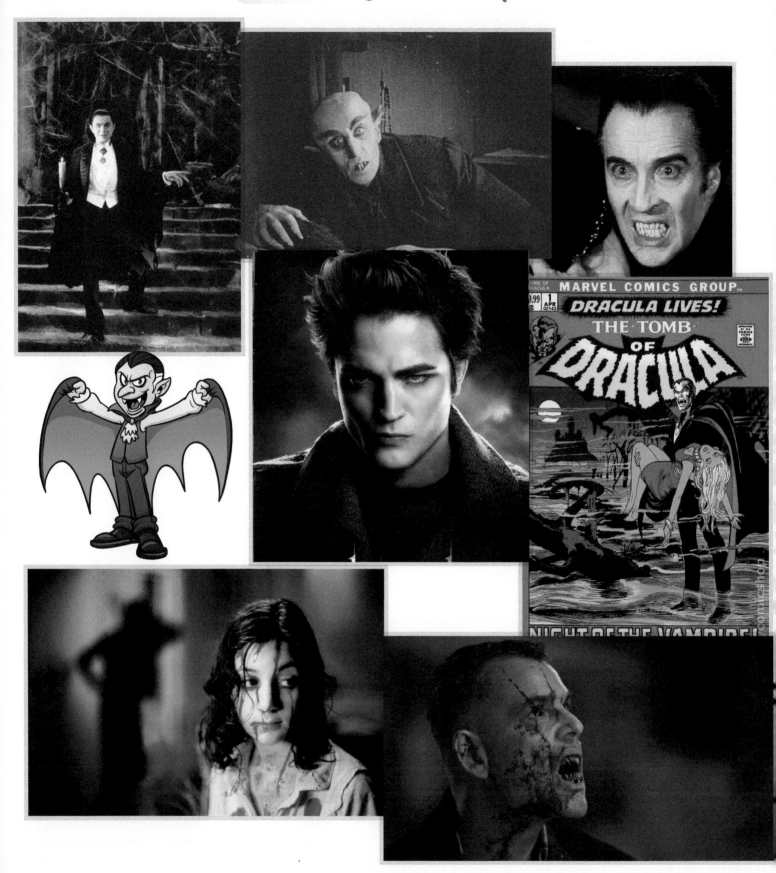

Text: analysing film posters

Film posters are one of the ways in which the film industry promotes a new film to an audience. They are used to persuade an audience to go and see a film. A good poster will give the information quickly to an audience. Posters often appear on billboards, in cinemas and in magazines and newspapers. An audience will not spend a long time looking at the poster so the words and images must make an immediate impact and be easily remembered. Posters will often attract an audience by including enigmas, an audience can only find the answers if they come and see the film. The poster will also introduce images and a tagline which will appear in other marketing material for the film. **Teaser campaigns** are a bit different and give less information.

Conventions of film posters

These will include:

- Clues to the film's genre – it is important that an audience knows which genre the film belongs to, for example horror or romantic comedy.

- Iconography – the objects, settings and costumes are further clues to the genre of a film.

- Stars – big name stars will also give a clue to the genre and what to expect from the film. Stars are often linked to certain types of film, for example Tom Cruise tends to appear in action films, and Reese Witherspoon in romantic comedies.

- The tagline – this is the memorable phrase or slogan that appears on all the marketing material and sums up the film.

What do the following taglines suggest about the films?

- Unleash the power behind the armour
- They have one chance to save us all
- Never take off the mask
- They'll do anything for their families, except grow up
- Everyone needs a little sunshine in their life
- He's still dead, but he's getting warmer

- The main image – this usually takes up most of the poster. It may tell the audience something about the genre, characters or the narrative.

Key Terms

Enigma
This is a puzzle or mystery contained in the text. A film poster or trailer, for example, will only give snippets of narrative, not the whole story, in the hope that the audience will want to come and see the film to find out the rest.

Teaser campaign
This is where there are several posters for the film. Each one gives a little bit more information running up to the film's release. Teaser posters use enigmas to catch the attention of the audience.

Why are film posters important in the marketing of a new film?

Task

What does the poster for *Brides of Dracula* tell the audience about the film? How do we know that this is a poster for an older vampire film?

85

the twilight saga
new moon

'TWILIGHT FOR GROWN-UPS
...A MUST SEE'
MTV NEWS

★★★★ ★★★★
SFX   RADIO TIMES

'TEN OUT OF TEN...
SERIOUSLY SCARY'
ALAN FRANK, DAILY STAR

★★★★ ★★★★
EMPIRE   VIRGIN MOVIES

Key Terms

Franchise
An entire series of the film including the original film and all those that follow on.

Hyperbole
This is over-exaggerated language that makes the film seem very good.

Production values
These are the elements of the film that tell the audience how much it cost to make. A film with high production values will include big name stars, expensive locations or special effects.

Tip

Using the correct media terms in your annotation will show your understanding.

- The name of the film – this will give a clue to the genre and the audience will know what to expect. The film may be part of a series and will use the name of the original plus a new name to suggest the film is different. Here the name *New Moon* links to the idea of werewolves so shows that it is part of the *Twilight* **franchise**.

- Language – this will aim to persuade an audience to go and see the film by telling them how good it is and what to expect. Sometimes **hyperbole** is used.

- Quotes – film posters will include quotes from newspapers and film magazines praising the film. This makes the audience think that they must go and see it. The poster may also feature a rating in the form of stars to suggest it is high quality.

- Quality mark – this is where the poster will include something that suggests the film is of a high quality, for example 'from the director of....' and naming a high profile film, or the logo from a famous film company.

FROM NEIL JORDAN
THE DIRECTOR OF
INTERVIEW WITH
THE VAMPIRE

Independent research

Brides of Dracula was made by Hammer Films. Find out what you can about this film company and their links to the vampire/horror genre.

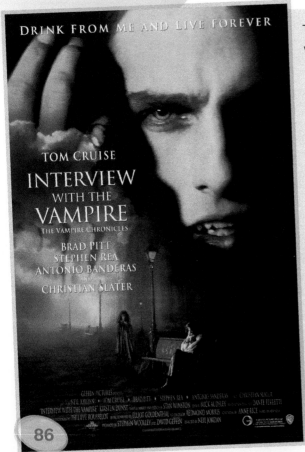

The tagline gives a clue to the film genre. 'Drink From Me' suggests a vampire's love of blood. 'Live Forever' suggests that vampires never die.

The main image takes up most of the poster. It is the face of the vampire with recognisable features – the pale skin, piercing eyes and pointed teeth. He is looking straight at the audience and half his face is in darkness, which gives a clue to his role in the film.

The big name stars are given billing, showing that this film has high **production values**. They are known to a range of audiences.

The name of the film clearly places it in the vampire/horror genre. It may suggest that another character gets close to a vampire by the use of the word 'interview'. This is an enigma – it may persuade the audience to go and see the film to find out what happens.

The clothing, setting and the object of the old street lamp are old-fashioned and tell the audience that it is not set in modern times. The overall colour of the poster also tells us this, it is like the colour of an old photograph.

The low key lighting makes the setting seem sinister.

The second, smaller image gives some clues to the narrative and the characters that may be involved in the film.

TASK

Choose a poster for a vampire/horror film and annotate it using the example on page 86 to help you.

TASK

Explore these film posters which are taken from different times. Comment on them using the following questions and the example to help you:

Images – why have they been chosen and what do they tell the audience about the film?

Layout and design – how have the posters been constructed to appeal to the audience?

Iconography – what do the objects and backgrounds used in the posters tell the audience about the film?

Graphics – how have the font styles and illustrations been used to give clues to the genre?

Persuasive techniques – what other aspects of the posters would persuade an audience to go and see the film?

TASK

Design a film poster for a new vampire horror film using some of the ideas from these posters to sell your film to an audience.

Evaluate your finished product explaining the techniques you have used to market your new film to an audience.

Text: analysing film trailers

Film trailers are another way to market a film to audiences. The aim of a film trailer is to give enough information, but not too much, so that the audience want to go and see the film.

Conventions of film trailers – an audience expects to see certain elements in a film trailer. These include:

- The name of the film. This is obviously important as the audience need to recognise the film later. The name of the film may give a clue to its genre, for example *The Vampire Diaries*. If the film is a sequel then the name usually links to the original film, for example *Twilight: Breaking Dawn.*

- The main characters. The characters and an extract showing their role in the film is a typical convention of a trailer. If they are played by high profile stars then the name may go alongside the shot of the character on the screen.

- The **tagline**. This will give the audience a clue to the genre and sometimes the narrative of the film.

- On-screen graphics. Words appear on the screen during the trailer. These may be the names of characters, stars or the tagline. The font style chosen will also help to tell the audience what sort of film it is.

- Enigmas. The purpose of a trailer is to make the audience want to go and see the film. The trailer will be put together to include some of the best bits of the film but leaves out bits of information so that the audience will have to go and see the film to find out what happens.

- Audio codes. The film trailer will include music, for example a theme tune that is used in all marketing for the film. It may be a recognisable song. There may also be music that gives a clue to the action, for example sinister music to show that an evil character is on screen. The trailer may also include sound effects that link to the genre, for example screams or the howling of wolves in a vampire/ horror film. A voice-over is usually used to explain some of the storyline to the audience. This tells the audience what to expect from the film.

- Technical codes – the trailer will use a range of camera shots and angles to hold the interest of the audience. The shots will be **edited** together to show the audience the storyline and make the trailer interesting. The pace of the trailer will link to the genre – an action film will be fast and dramatic, a suspense thriller may be slower and more thoughtful.

- Editing – the aim of the trailer is to catch the attention of the audience. In a trailer, scenes from the film are chosen in order to introduce the narrative and the characters. These are put together to create an effect and are often accompanied

Key Term

Tagline
This is the short phrase or slogan that appears in trailers and on posters. It gives a clue to the genre and storyline of the film and often includes an enigma.

Editing
In the production of a film, film-makers will have a lot of footage to choose from. Editing is the way in which the shots and scenes from a film are put together to make a full length film or a trailer.

Quickfire 50

What does the font style for *Bram Stoker's Dracula* suggest about the film?

by music, sound effects or a voice-over to help the scenes make sense to the audience. It is sometimes the case that a good trailer that is edited well can make the film seem more interesting than it actually is.

Tip

When you are investigating a text like a film trailer, remember to use the correct media language.

Task

Look at the stills taken from the vampire horror film *Byzantium* (2012). What different conventions of a film trailer can be seen in these images? What else would you expect to be included in this trailer?

Quickfire
51

Why are trailers important in the marketing of a film?

Text and organisations: investigating film and television extracts

Now you need to investigate some film extracts to explore whether the conventions of the vampire horror film have changed over time. You will find that some films, particularly those with a focus on the character of Dracula, have kept some of the conventions of the film. Other film producers have realised that audiences have a fascination with the vampire genre and have just adapted the ideas in order to appeal to a new generation.

By exploring some key scenes from a range of films and television programmes you will see that there are similarities even though some of the films were made years apart. You can then contrast the older films with films and television programmes that have introduced more modern versions of the vampire. This will help you to prepare for a Textual investigation based on this topic. Here are some examples.

Quickfire 52

Why do you think that the producers of films would choose to keep some of the ideas from the early films and the book in more modern film versions?

Tip

The films investigated here are suggestions – you can choose examples of your own to investigate. You need to be able to transfer the skills you have learned to any text.

Extract I: *Nosferatu*

It is interesting to look at an extract from this film as it was one of the earliest representations of the vampire in film. It may look dated now but, even though it was a silent film, it scared the audience of the time. This film can be found on YouTube: http://tinyurl.com/cu5xzm

- How is this early representation of a vampire different from what we now expect?
- Do you think it is still scary? How?
- How are the other characters in the film represented? For example, the young woman who becomes the vampire's victim?
- Is the film still effective even though it is silent? How?

Extract 2: Bela Lugosi in *Dracula* (1931)

This was the film that introduced the character of Dracula with the appearance we recognise today; the long black cloak, medallion, white face and slicked black hair. Look at the early scenes in the film where the clerk makes the journey in a coach to the inn and changes coaches. Despite warnings from fellow travellers, he then goes on to Dracula's castle and first meets Dracula. Whilst there he cuts his finger on a paper knife and Dracula has to restrain himself when he sees the blood. This narrative is very true to the original story.

- What can you say about the iconography used in these scenes?
- How is the audience introduced to the setting?
- How do the audio codes help to create an eerie atmosphere?
- What typical conventions of the vampire/horror genre appear in this film?

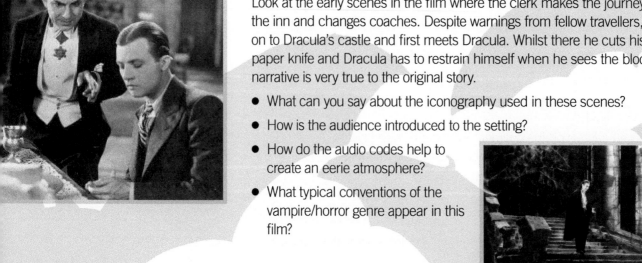

Extract 3: *Bram Stoker's Dracula*

This film was made in 1992 and whilst it includes some typical conventions of the genre, it also modernises it. Look at scenes including the journey of the clerk to Dracula's castle and his meeting with the vampire.

- How are these scenes from the film similar to those from *Dracula* (1931)?
- How are iconography and special effects used to establish the film's genre?
- What can you say about the representation of Dracula here?

Extract 4: *Twilight*

This is an interesting film to explore as it re-introduced the genre to a new, young audience and was a huge success. The idea also came from a book. However, this film is more of a hybrid genre. In the film the vampire is different in that Edward Cullen is not happy being a vampire and his aim in the film is to not kill humans.

One scene to explore is Chapter 2 First Day At School:

- In what ways is this scene similar to one you might see in a teen 'high school' film?
- What does the audience learn about The Cullens? How is Jessica's role in the narrative similar to the villagers in other films of this genre?
- How are The Cullens represented as being 'different'? How do the technical and audio codes help to establish this representation?

Another useful scene is Chapters 11/12 How Long Have You Been 17?

Here Bella, who is suspicious of Edward, has done some research into vampires. In her research the audience are shown more recognisable representations of vampires and their features and habits, for example drinking the blood of humans. She then confronts Edward.

- What does the audience learn about Edward Cullen in these scenes?
- How is he similar to and different from the representations of vampires in the extracts from other films you have watched?
- How do the technical codes and setting add to the representation?

Key Figure

Hammer Horror
Other interesting film texts include the vampire horror films produced by this British film company Hammer Films. These were made from the mid-1950s to the 1970s and were very successful. There were several films made with the vampire theme focusing on the battle between Dracula and the vampire slayer Van Helsing.

QUICKfire 53

Why is it important to make the character of Dracula interesting?

QUICKfire 54

How has *Twilight* tried to attract a new audience to the vampire genre?

Vampires on television

In order to demonstrate that this topic area crosses several media forms you could also examine a television programme, for example *Being Human* and explore how it represents vampires.

Key Term

Opening sequence
This is the beginning of the film where the genre, characters, setting and storyline are introduced.

Task

Look at the trailers for *Being Human*, a television programme from the vampire genre aired on BBC3 for five series:

http://tinyurl.com/36asny8

● What common conventions of vampire films can you spot?
● What is different?
● Who do you think is the target audience for this programme and how have they been attracted?

Tip

For another text presented across different forms look at the website for *Being Human*:
http://tinyurl.com/7yoxott
There was also a spin-off web drama linked to the series called *Becoming Human* featuring one of the characters. This was a marketing device to keep viewers interested between series of the programme.

Tip

Don't be too ambitious, simple shots and editing are often more effective.

Media texts: practice production assignment

Production brief

To produce a short **opening sequence** or a trailer for a new vampire film or television programme demonstrating your understanding of the codes and conventions of this genre. You will work in small groups (no larger than 4).

Points to consider

You will need to demonstrate your understanding of the main codes and conventions of this genre that you have learned by exploring examples of films and television programmes:

Narrative – how will you introduce the storyline of your film/television programme?

Characters – what character types will you include?

Setting and iconography – this will need some careful thought!

Technical codes – what types of shots will you use in order to make your film/TV programme effective? It may be best to concentrate on creating suspense and tension through the use of close-ups and medium shots.

Audio codes – how will you use music and sound effects to enhance your moving image? If you are intending to record dialogue, you will need to plan how best to do this.

You will need to produce

- A storyboard of your short extract. Be clear about what you need to include in a storyboard and remember that a storyboard is a print record of your moving image. Try to discuss the shots in your film to see if they will work before drawing the storyboard. Think about building tension through close-ups and tight editing. Use the template on page 119 to help you and to ensure you include everything you need.

- A short opening sequence or trailer demonstrating your ability to use generic conventions and showing your technical competence. If you are working in group, it is important that everyone has a technical role, for example, filming, editing or sound.

- An evaluative report discussing genre conventions, representations, narrative, audience and organisations.

Key Term

Convergence
This is the way in which one topic can be presented across different media forms.

Audio-visual Textual investigation: genre

Investigate how far (your chosen texts) conform to genre conventions.

- Discuss extracts from two films and refer briefly to another different text (e.g. a film poster or a TV programme) in your investigation. This will demonstrate your awareness of **convergence** in the media.

- You can present your work as a written essay. You can use images/screen shots in your work, e.g. you can find an image from the programme or film and annotate it to show your understanding of genre conventions.

- You can present your work as a PowerPoint presentation incorporating annotated images, bullet pointed information, etc. Your work must be 400–850 words in length.

Use the following to help you to plan your work.

Introduction

Explain what you expect to see (the conventions) in any horror/vampire film. Explain where the first ideas came from and how some of the conventions can still be seen in modern texts. Think about:

- Characters
- Setting and iconography
- Narrative.

Explain which main text you will use and which extracts you will be discussing. Which other text will you refer to as a contrast?

Tip

If you are working in a group, make sure that everyone knows what their role is, for example filming a particular scene, making sure the sound is right, etc.

Tip

If you choose to present your investigation as a PowerPoint you must ensure that you still demonstrate analytical skills and meet the word length.

Tip

Back up what you say with specific examples from your texts. It should be clear that you have explored your examples in detail.

Key Term

Conform
This means following the rules of the vampire horror genre and including all or most of the main conventions that are shared by similar films.

Tip
Check your work against the Success criteria; this will help you to check you have included what you need to in your work.

Tip
When exploring technical and audio codes, always say why the shot or angle has been used and think about the possible effect this may have on the audience.

Tip
Choosing two texts that have some differences will make them easier to compare.

Tip
Remember to consider the impact of the organisations and how they may use genre conventions to market their products.

Text 1

You will need to answer the question and explore whether the film you have chosen **conforms** to the genre conventions, e.g. *Dracula*, or if it is different, e.g. *Twilight*.

Now comment on:

- **Characters** – are they what we expect to see in this genre or are they different? You can find an image from the film and annotate it to make your points clearer. Can you briefly compare this film with another from the same genre?
- **Setting and iconography** – how do we know we are watching the vampire/horror genre? What examples of settings, props, clothing, etc., are there to suggest this genre? Can you briefly compare this film with another from the same genre? You can include an image and annotate it.
- **Technical and audio codes** – give examples of any camera shots, angles, editing techniques or any sounds that are conventions of this genre. Remember to say how and why they have been used. Can you briefly compare this film with another from the same genre?
- **Narrative** – explain what happens in the story and if it is conventional for this genre. Some elements may be the same, for example the coach ride to Dracula's castle; others may be different, for example the appearance of the vampire. Try not to tell the story; try to explore how it fits into the genre. Can you briefly compare this film with another from the same genre?
- **Audience** – how do the genre conventions attract and appeal to an audience?

Conclusion

Answer the initial question. How far does the main film you have discussed conform to genre conventions? Is it similar to other films of the same genre or does it do something different? Support what you say by comparing it briefly with the other text(s) you mentioned.

Success criteria

Lower Level 3

- You have explored the way in which your texts conform to vampire horror genre conventions in some detail.
- You have shown awareness of the ways in which audiences can be attracted to the text because of its typical genre conventions.
- You have referred to more than one text.
- You have used some media vocabulary in your investigation.
- You have organised your investigation and shown your understanding of genre.

Lower Level 4

- You have shown an excellent ability to analyse the way in which your texts conform to vampire horror genre conventions in some detail.
- You have shown an awareness of both the audience and the organisations that produced the text.
- You have confidently used a wide range of media terms.
- Your writing and presentation are coherent and very accurate.

9: Music

Exploring Music as a topic in your GCSE course will allow you to investigate a selection of print and audio-visual texts from a range of different media forms and platforms including:

- Music magazines
- CD covers
- Music videos
- Industry and fan websites.

Each of these texts can be explored using the Media Studies Framework: text, organisations and audience. In exploring this topic you will also practise your analytical and production skills.

Introductory activities

- Write a list of all the different music genres you can think of, for example hip-hop and folk. For each genre think of the artists/bands who would fit into that genre. Are there some performers who belong to more than one genre?

- Think of three words that would best sum up each genre.

- Choose one music genre. Put together a mood board/collage of images which you think represents that genre. This may include images of artists, CD covers, font styles or particular colours.

- Look at the review section of a newspaper, magazine or website that features new releases. Consider how the images used and the description of the music give the audience information about the music genre.

The music industry, just like any other media industry, uses a range of media platforms to market itself and the texts it produces. It needs to make sure that information about new and existing bands and artists gets out to the target audience so that the fans will buy the music, concert tickets and merchandise and so make money for the industry.

Media texts: music magazines

Music magazines are one of the ways in which the music industry markets its performers. Music magazines are a sub-genre of magazines and specific magazines often focus on a particular music genre. They therefore are trying to attract a **niche audience** rather than a **mainstream audience**.

Key Terms

Niche audience
With regard to music magazines, this means a small audience with a specific interest in a music sub-genre. For example, the target audience of *Total Guitar* magazine is those people who are interested in both playing the guitar and reading about artists who play this instrument.

Mainstream audience
This is a broad target audience. Here, a magazine would try to include lots of different genres of music and artists in order to appeal to as many people as possible.

What is the advantage to a music magazine of having a niche target audience? Are there any disadvantages?

What is the aim of a music magazine front cover?

- To attract the target audience.
- To have a **masthead** that suggests the genre and is recognisable to an audience.
- To establish the **house style** of the magazine so that it will be recognisable to readers.
- To clearly establish the music genre of the magazine through content and images.
- To stand out from other similar magazines.
- To attract the reader through the strong central image. This image will usually be of an artist or band belonging to the magazine's music genre and will be easily recognised by the target audience.
- To use language that reinforces the music genre of the magazine. For example, names of performers.
- To make the reader feel that the magazine is for them.
- To offer extra reasons for the reader to buy this particular magazine instead of another one. **Sell lines** are used to attract audiences.
- To suggest to the reader that they have the most up-to-date news and information about the artists and bands that are popular with the target audience.

Key Terms

Masthead
This is the title of the magazine. The name and font style may give a clue to the genre. For example,

House style
This is the 'look' of the magazine that makes it different from other magazines. This may be the font style, the language, mode of address, layout and design or the colours used.

Sell lines
This is the information on the cover that tells the reader what extra they can get if they buy the magazine. They usually 'sell' competitions and free gifts.

How does *Vibe* magazine establish its music genre on the front cover?

Text: genre – analysing music magazines

The masthead gives a clue to the magazine's rock music genre. The central image is placed over the title, this suggests that the magazine is well known. The title links to the sound made when playing a power chord on an electric guitar.

The central image is of an 'of the minute' band who belongs to the rock music genre. Although they are dressed formally one of them has lip piercings and a visible tattoo suggesting rebellion.

The **mode of address** of the artists is direct and the code of expression of one of the artists is aggressive.

The **cover lines** link to the genre and target the audience who likes this music. Only fans of this music genre will recognise the names of the bands and artists, this makes the buyer of the magazine feel part of the magazine's community.

The sell lines tell the prospective reader that they can 'Win!' and get something free.

This issue came out around Valentine's Day 2014 so it includes language related to this day – 'your dates for this issue', 'random date generator'.

The use of lightning bolts and exclamation marks make the magazine seem dramatic and reflect the music genre. Even the graphic hearts are broken in two!

The layout and design is informal, the images of the music artists down the side are presented as snapshots and they all have a direct mode of address making them look natural and not constructed. This reflects the **house style** of the magazine.

The colour scheme is bold and catches the eye.

The banner along the bottom uses exaggerated language to persuade you to buy the magazine.

We Love Pop is a magazine from a different music genre and targets a different audience from Kerrang!

Quickfire 57

We Love Pop is a new magazine and was published when sales for print magazines were falling. Why do you think it has been successful?

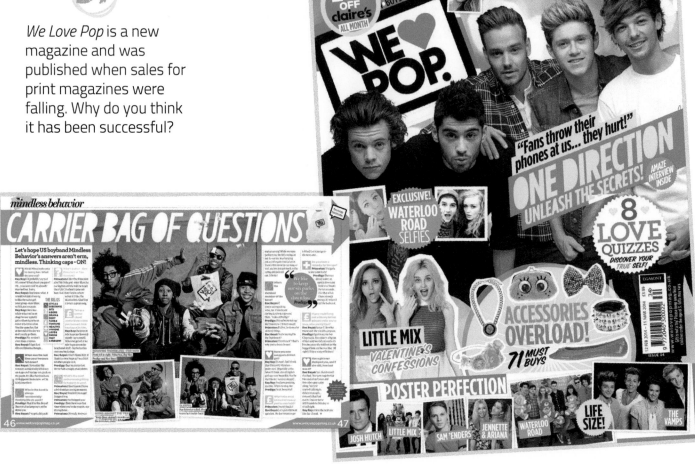

TASK

Investigate the front cover of this or a similar magazine of your own choice commenting on:

- The use of colour.
- The layout and design.
- The genre conventions of this style of magazine.
- The cover lines – what do they tell the audience about the magazine's genre?
- The choice of images – how have the artists/bands been represented by the magazine?
- The target audience and how they have been attracted to the magazine.

TASK

Obviously it is not just the front cover of the magazine that is important. It is the shop window, but what is inside is equally important.

Choose a music magazine and select a double-page spread from inside the magazine. Use the points from the We Love Pop task to investigate how the pages attract the target audience.

The magazine industry

This industry is very big and powerful. All magazines are owned by a few major publishers. They make a lot of money from all the titles they own so they can afford to produce some niche magazines that may not make much profit. The main magazine publishers are:

Bauer Media – this company owns over 300 magazine titles including *Kerrang!*, *MOJO* and *Q*.

IPC Media – this company is part of the Time Warner company and publishes several titles including *NME* Magazine.

Smaller publishers produce other music titles including *We Love Pop* (Egmont UK), *Vibe* (Spin Media), *Rolling Stone* (Jann Wenner).

Top of The Pops magazine is a BBC publication.

Practice production assignment: music magazines

Create the front cover and contents page for a new music magazine aimed at a teenage audience.

Research

- Annotate examples of front covers of music magazines similar to the one you want to create.
- Conduct some audience research; this could be a questionnaire or a focus group.
- Research the websites of magazine publishers and their media packs.
- Investigate the companies who publish music magazines similar to the one you want to create. How do they market their products? Which companies advertise in these magazines? How much does it cost for a full-page advert?

Planning

- Create a mood board of ideas. This may include font styles, colours, examples of interesting layouts, etc.
- Mock up a front cover and contents page.
- Take a range of photographs for the two pages. Annotate the ones you want to use and the ones you have rejected, explaining your decisions.

Production

Create your front cover and contents page. Try to make it look as professional as you can using the software you have in your school.

Evaluation

Discuss your final product considering how you have met your aims, used genre conventions, used representation and narrative, showed awareness of organisational issues and attracted your target audience.

Tip

Although this is a practice assignment, many students choose to produce magazine pages for their final GCSE production piece. What worked well and what went wrong will help you to gain the skills you need.

Tip

It is important to be aware of the industry that produces the media text. Investigating the industry can be one of your research items for your final production assignment.

Tip

When you are annotating examples, remember to use the correct media terms.

Text: narrative – analysing music videos

Just like music magazines, music videos are another way in which the music industry markets performers and their music. Many music videos made today have **high production values** and are therefore also entertaining to watch.

The purpose of a music video is to:

- Promote a single or an album.
- Promote the artist or band, or with an existing artist, remind the audience of who they are and their music.
- Create, adapt or feed into a **star image**.
- Entertain the audience.
- Set the 'meanings' of a song by the use of images and a story.

Music videos can feature the artist or band or they may include actors as part of the story. The main styles of music video are as follows.

Performance music video

The codes and conventions of performance music videos include:

- Close-ups of the artist or band 'performing', for example singing or playing instruments. Where artists are filmed playing instruments this is included to show that they are 'serious' musicians.
- The mode of address may be direct so that it seems to the audience that the artist is singing to them.
- Clips from concert performances. This also includes shots of the audience to make the viewer feel involved and want to be part of the live experience.
- To make the video more interesting the band/artist sometimes performs in unusual places, for example on the top of a cliff and will be **lip synched**.
- Shots of the band members/artist in more realistic, informal situations, for example singing on the tour bus or practising.

Key Terms

High production values
This means that the music video cost a lot to make. You can tell this is the case if the locations are exotic and the technical codes are more complex, for example shots from a helicopter.

Star image
This refers to the idea that stars want to communicate about themselves to the audience. For example, Lady Gaga uses interviews, public performances and her clothing as well as her music videos to show a specific image that keeps her fans interested.

Lip synch
This is where the lip movements of the singer are matched up with the vocals. This is usually done at the end when the video is being edited.

Quickfire 58

What codes and conventions of performance music videos can be seen in the stills from Little Mix and Coldplay?

Still from *Christmas Lights*, Coldplay

Still from *Move*, Little Mix

Narrative music video

In this style of music video the performer tells a story using the song lyrics. The main conventions of a narrative music video are:

- Telling the story of the song lyrics through technical codes and editing.

- A narrative may involve the performer or use actors to tell the story. For example, Ed Sheeran used Rupert Grint in his music video for *Lego House.* In Ellie Goulding's video for *I Know You Care*, she acts as the narrator but is separate from the story that is told by actors. The film cuts between them and Ellie Goulding singing. The video moves backward and forward in time and place and has an enigma at the end.

- The music video can be a short film with a clear narrative structure. It may use narrative techniques used in full length films, for example flashbacks.

- The characters used may be recognisable stereotypes as there isn't much time in a 3–4-minute music video to create more complex characters.

Tip

Revisit Section 2: Media Studies Framework where you can read about narrative techniques. This will help you to analyse the music videos.

Stills taken from *I Know You Care,* Ellie Goulding

Find an example of a narrative music video. Explore the techniques it uses to tell the story of the lyrics.

Task

Some music videos use a combination of performance and narrative techniques. In Olly Murs' music video for *Dear Darlin'* he performs, playing the guitar and singing on the roof of a building. He also acts in the narrative, at times the story goes on around him as he sings. This makes the story seem more personal to the audience and makes the story seem as if it really happened.

Quickfire 59

How do music videos help create the star's image?

Stills taken from *Dear Darlin',* Olly Murs

Storyboard a music video for an existing music track. You will be more creative if you choose a track that does not already have a video made. Try to include some of the techniques discussed in this chapter.

Key Term

Insert
This is the small booklet that comes inside the CD. It may contain more images of the band/artist, artwork and song lyrics.

Text: analysing CD covers

Another marketing device used by the music industry is the CD cover and the **insert** that goes with it. It is one of the ways in which an artist can introduce themselves to a new audience and can help to create their star image. It is also one of the texts that the artist may have more control over in terms of how they are represented. Although the sales of CDs have fallen as music fans use other digital means to download and listen to their music, CDs are still produced and sold by artists.

Independent research

Design an audience questionnaire to find out whether music fans still buy CDs or listen to music in other ways.

The conventions of CD covers

CD covers are a recognisable print text as they have a clear set of codes and conventions:

- A central image. This may be a photograph of the artist or band. If this is the case, the mode of address is usually direct in order to relate to the fan. The music artist will have decided how they want to be represented through the images chosen.

- Iconography. The CD cover may include objects and backgrounds that give clues to the music genre. For example, 'bling' objects in a rap CD or particular musical instruments for a rock CD.

- Layout and design. CD covers are always a set size. Included on the front cover will be the name of the artist and the CD, the font style and colours chosen will communicate messages about the performer and the music. The 'Parental Advisory' sticker will be visible as a warning about the contents of the lyrics.

- The back cover. This will usually have less information but, importantly, will have the names of the tracks. This information is important as the fans may buy the CD on the strength of the singles released already. They then know what they are going to get. The song titles can also give a clue to the music genre.

- Clues to genre. The front and back covers of a CD will tell an audience what the music genre is through codes of clothing, objects, gesture and expression.

Tip

Questionnaires can be used as one of the research elements of your final production piece. It is important to practise the types of questions that allow you to get the information you need.

How does the 'Parental Advisory' sticker work as a form of regulation?

Tip

Revisit Section 2: Media Studies Framework to remind yourself what is meant by representation as a media term.

TASK

Investigate how the CD covers for Katy Perry and 50 cent suggest the music genre and construct a **representation** of the artist. Comment on:

- The central image
- Layout and design
- Iconography
- Images
- Visual and technical codes.

Key Term

Representation
With regard to the music industry, you can use the texts we have discussed in this chapter to investigate how the representation of gender, age, ethnicity and place is constructed by the music industry.

Practice planning task

Design a mock-up for a CD cover for a new artist belonging to a specific genre of your choice.

Annotate your design to explain the decisions you have made and how you have represented the music genre and the artist/band.

Text: analysing music websites

Websites are another way in which performers market their music and themselves. They are different from the other texts explored in this chapter as they allow the user to be more interactive. They have to work harder to attract the attention of the audience and they have to offer them reasons to come back for more. There are two main types of music website related to a performer, the official site and the sites created by fans. There will be only one official site, but there may be several fan sites for one artist/band.

Conventions of official music websites

- Official band websites must be appealing, inviting and of course pleasing to the eye. The aim is to attract users who in turn will browse through the site, listen to the material and convert to loyal fans.
- It is also important in some cases that the design of the website reflects the genre of the music in its iconography, colour and features.
- Information. This may include: concert dates, press releases and 'inside information' and 'gossip' linked to the band/artist. This serves to make the user feel they are more informed and involved with the band.

- Multimedia features. These may include: video footage of the band in concert, interviews with the artist/band members and a photo gallery. The images may appear in a banner and may change as the user 'rolls over' the image. There will be links to social networking sites – Twitter, Facebook, for example, and opportunities to listen to music.

- **Interactive opportunities.** These will include chances to email the artist, contribute to blogs, choose particular videos to watch, etc.

- **Merchandise.** Opportunities to buy T-shirts, posters, caps and other band memorabilia to show you are a real fan!

- Industry links. Links to other websites, record companies, merchandising companies, etc. This may include some external advertising – this is one way the site will make money.

- Navigational features. These are the features that help the audience/user to move easily around the website.

Key Terms

Interactive opportunities
This refers to the different ways in which the user of the site can actually become involved.

Merchandise
These are the performer-related products that you can buy, they may be exclusive to the website.

TASK

What codes and conventions of music websites are there on the *One Direction* official site?
http://www.onedirectionmusic.com/gb/home/

TASK

Compare an official and a fan website for the same artist/band. How do they both promote the artist/band and appeal to an audience?

What are the main differences between official and fan music sites?

Music: Textual investigations

As this is such a broad topic there are a range of Textual investigations that you can complete. Here is one suggestion.

Explore how the narrative is constructed in (name of two music videos).

You must:

- Discuss two music videos in your investigation. One will be your main focus and the second will be referred to in less detail.
- You can use images in your work, e.g. you can find an image from the music video and annotate it to show your understanding of conventions.
- Focus on narrative – how the story is told.
- Your work must be 400–850 words in length.

Introduction

Explain the purpose of a music video. What different styles of music video are there? Explain which main text you will use and which other texts you will refer to.

Main focus

Now use the videos you have chosen to comment on:

- Setting and iconography – how do they help to convey the narrative?
- Technical and audio codes – give examples of any camera shots, angles, editing techniques or any sounds that are conventions of a narrative music video. Can you briefly compare this with another narrative music video? How do the technical codes 'tell the story'?
- Narrative – explain how what happens in the story is conventional for this genre. Try not to describe, try to analyse. Can you briefly compare this music video with another music video?
- What other codes and conventions are used in the music videos to communicate the narrative?
- Audience – what techniques have been used to attract the target audience of your videos?
- Organisations – consider why music videos are important marketing tools. How have your examples helped to promote the artist(s)?

Conclusion

Answer the initial question.

- Sum up how the narrative is constructed in the music videos you have chosen to analyse.
- Refer to audience and organisations.

> **Tip**
>
> Make sure that you have the correct combination of Textual investigations to submit for your GCSE. Other investigations you could complete for this topic are:
>
> Explore how genre conventions are used in CD covers.
>
> Explore how far the representation of gender in music websites reinforces conventional points of view.

10: Controlled Assessment – Approaching Production

Tip

Take note of the mark allocations for the different elements of the production. This will help you to plan your time – the production is worth the most marks and so should have the greatest amount of time spent on it. It is easy to get carried away with planning and research activities and not leave enough time for the production!

This is part of your Controlled Assessment which, combined with your two Textual investigations is 60% of your final mark. The production must not be based on the examination topic or the topics chosen for the Textual investigations. If you are producing an audio-visual text you can work as part of a group. If your text is print you must work on your own.

TASK

Research, plan and create a media product and evaluate this product.

This task is made up of four elements:

✓	Research	10 marks
✓	Planning	10 marks
✓	Production	50 marks
✓	Evaluation	10 marks

Tip

Make sure that your audience research is focused and useful. Focus groups where you bring a group of interested people together to discuss your ideas are usually more useful than handing out lots of questionnaires.

Research (10 marks)

You must show evidence of research consisting of *a minimum of two pieces and a maximum of four pieces*. Research methods that can be used include:

- Textual annotation, e.g. annotating a magazine cover similar to the style of the one you want to create, exploring the key features.
- Audience research including, for example, focus groups, questionnaires, surveys, electronic bulletin boards and blogs.
- Research into media organisations including, for example, the production and distribution of similar texts, e.g. film and TV companies, advertising agencies.
- Research into budgets and production costs of your chosen texts.

You must not present the same findings as other students even if you are working as part of a group.

Higher marks are gained by clear explanations of how the findings of your research have been used in the final production and by using media terminology appropriate to your chosen text.

Tip

Use the planning sheet on page 118 to help you to structure your ideas.

Examples of research

Masthead-

At the top of the page so can be seen in magazine racks. Bold writing to stand out, but due to the older more sophisticated target audience of 4-4-2, it's quite a basic font.

Background-

Basic so the attention is on the image and content teasers.

Colours-

The colours here connote football. The background is green just like a football pitch, with white text on the masthead which looks like the sidelines to a football pitch. Also, the background to the main text on the cover is red and yellow, just like red and yellow cars used in a football game.

Text-

There is teasers to attract readers interested in the topic. Bold sub headings to attract attention and then a bit of extra text underneath giving a brief description on the article.

This is seen a lot on magazines and will appear on mine.

Code of Clothing-

Training kit, shows informality as the purpose of Frank being in the magazine is to entertain as well as inform. The training kit is also a convention of football so this follows what you would expect to see on the magazine. Quite sophisticated colour of clothing to appeal to target audience, unlike a magazine for young children which may contain brighter colours.

4-4-2 Media Pack-

Predominant audience is males and 52% of their audience is aged between 25 and 44. A huge majority of it's readers work full time. Every year their readers spend more than £100 on

Anchorage-

Text to go with the main image.

Comment

Analysing examples of existing texts similar to the one you want to create is one of the most popular forms of research. This method of research also gives you the chance to show that you can use media terminology.

Here you can see that the students have commented on lots of key features of the text including layout and design, visual codes and anchorage. There is also a comment about the audience, showing that the student knows that appealing to the target audience is important.

'shout' is aimed at teens unlike 'heat' which is aimed at a older audience. Although they have different target audiences they both have a lot of conventions alike each other as they are both celebrity magazines and are sending the same message however in a different way. For example the teens magazine has a lot less writing on the front cover. As this magazine is aimed at teens and 'heat' is aimed at a older audience, im going to use them both to help me create my magazine. The magazine I am producing will nor be aimed at a older or a teen audience but will just have a overall appeal to females. Annotating and analysing both will help me to create a understanding in what a celebrity magazines need to become successful.

On this particular magazine it is clearly shown that the target audience is teenagers. The bold writing makes the magazine appear less formal and allows it to stand out as the background to it contrasts with the distinctive font.

Typically girls like to discuss things and talk about boys. This magazine allows the audience to do so, featuring boys can engage the audience to read the magazine. The boys featured are used in a masculine way and as a sex object as they are described as 'hot'

masculine way and as a sex object as they are described as 'hot' again relating to the 'slang' used. On the front cover it states that the 'lads' are 'rated and slated' these ratings will be an opinion therefore this can include the audience by allowing them to read it and debate the opinions given. This tool is used to get the audience involved and allow them to feel like they have a connection with the magazine. Aswell as this other things are featured to do with males such as 'is you male real or fake' thjis being a question can engage the reader to open the magazine and want to know the answer. This topic can appeal to teens

Another thing that makes the magazine clearly aimed at teens is the 'slang' terms used such as 'lads' being used as a replacement of other things which could have been possibly used, such as 'males' or 'men' . This is used to appeal to the target audience as they can relate to it and form a connection between there lifestyle and the magazine. This is an effective way to connect to the audience. As my magazine only has a target audience of women this technique would be used throughout the magazine however not on the front cover so that it repells the older audience from reading the magazine.

The model used on the main part of the magqzine is the thing that stands out the most, code of address is clearly shownt hrough the eye connection with the audience. The close up shot can allow code of expression to come across and allows the magazine to again, build a connection with the magazine.

Comment

The analysis of *shout* magazine is detailed and it very closely explores the purpose and effect of the features of the front page. There is a clear understanding of the target audience and the student makes close links between the language used and the target audience.

The research pictured here is linked to two different productions: a film trailer and an advertisement for a fragrance. The screen shots from the actual production text are included later in this section.

75% of the people asked said they didn't mind what gender the main character was. I thought this would be important to know as the audience seems to always connect more with the main character, so if there was a preferred gender I would have taken that into account and chose that character gender.

Would you prefer to see a male lead role or a female lead role?

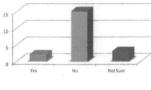

Most people said that they did not mind what gender the main character was, when asked to explain a few said similar things,

'It doesn't bother me who the lead character is as long as we get to know them and they have an interesting story'.

I took this into account when choosing my actors.

75% of people also said that it was a bad idea giving away lots of the storyline. They said *'it ruins the mystery'* and *'there's no point watching the film if it gives everything away in the the trailer'* So I know that I have to intrigue the audience in my trailer without giving too much away.

Do you think that it's good if a trailer gives away a lot of the storyline?

Marc Jacobs 'Daisy'

This close up shot is used in the commercial to highlight the emotion of the model, allowing the audience to view the ad. as relatable. It also conveys the mode of adress is 'direct', portraying the 'natural' and 'real' theme and tone of the advertisement.

The code of clothing (underwear) emphasises the

models feminity, portraying the target audience of women who would find this relatable or possibly something to envy. The setting highlights the womens connection to the earth, imply the natural theme of the product.

The shot of the girls backs adds intrigue for the audience, reflecting the interest in the smell of the perfume. The low angle shot implies feminine strength and power, which women may find relatable, therefore be more likely to appreciate the product.

Tip
Using media terminology demonstrates a more sophisticated ability to analyse.

Comment

The first two pieces here are examples of audience research. They both explore the findings from their research and link it directly to what they intend to produce. This allows you to be more analytical. This method is more useful than just including lots of questionnaires. The research into the trailer has also included direct quotes from the focus group and is used to support the production.

The research into the advertisement shown on page 110 focuses on the importance of music and images in appealing to audience. You can see clearly how this research has been used by the student later in their production.

The second focus of research is into existing products. Here the student has researched the advert for Marc Jacobs' *Daisy* fragrance as it is closely linked to the style she wants to create. The analysis mentions the use of shots, the mode of address and the ways in which the advertisement appeals to an audience.

Mood board
This is a collection of, for example, images, text, and fabrics that help to put together ideas for a production piece.

Recce
This refers to a pre-filming visit to possible locations to see if they are suitable for filming. Usually photographs will be taken to record the locations.

Planning (10 marks)

You must show evidence of planning approaches appropriate to your chosen production text – *a minimum of two and a maximum of four* planning techniques are required. Planning approaches may include:

- Scripts
- Storyboards
- **Mood/inspiration boards**
- Running orders and shot lists
- **Recce** information/images
- Mock-ups
- Experimenting with font styles, masthead ideas and photographs.

Higher marks are gained by clear explanations of how the techniques have been used to develop the final production and by using media terminology appropriate to your chosen text.

Examples of planning: a recce

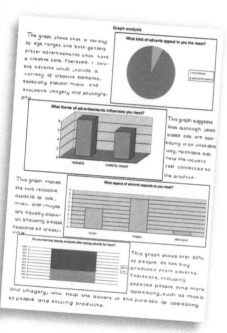

Tip

If you decide to create a mood board remember to annotate it or provide a commentary highlighting why you chose the items you included on it and how they will help with your production.

Commentary

Here is an example of how to present a recce. The students have taken pictures of possible locations to use in their productions. They have annotated the images, suggesting how they will be used and the effect they would have on the audience. It is a good example of how the same location, which may be near your school, can be used for different products.

The student producing the advert suggests how the locations will add to the image of the product.

In this way both students make clear links between the planning and the production.

Examples of planning: storyboards

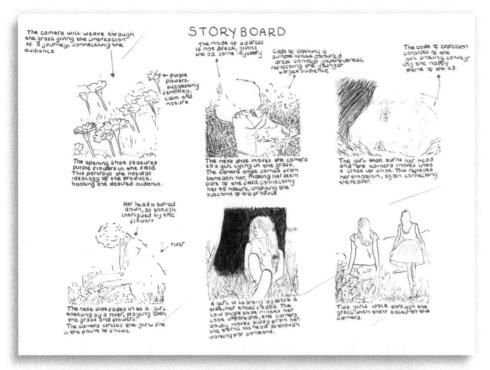

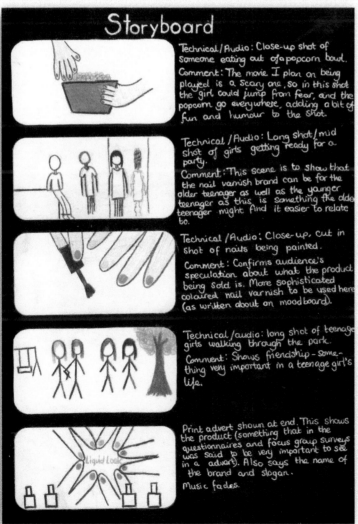

Commentary

Creating a storyboard is an essential planning task if you are producing an audio-visual piece. A storyboard is a good way of recording the camera shots, angles, movement and editing you can visualise in your head. You also need to indicate sound.

On a storyboard you will usually include details of the technical and audio codes. You may also comment, as these students have, on the reasons for including the shot and the effect of the shot on the audience.

Notice also how both students use the correct media terminology.

You can create your own storyboard template or your teacher may give you one to work from to ensure you include everything needed. There is an example of one you can use on page 119.

You should then use your storyboard as a guide when you film.

Tip

Imagining the film sequence as a moving image before you record it on a storyboard is important. This allows you to think about what will work visually and what won't.

Production (50 marks)

For this you will use your research and planning to create your own media text. This can be print or audio-visual. You will be given a list of options from which to choose.

You can work in small groups only if you are producing an audio-visual text. A group of three/four is ideal. All members of the group must have **clearly defined roles** as you will be assessed on your contribution to the finished product.

Higher marks can be gained for an original approach to the production rather than just copying an existing example.

You must use your own images wherever possible – this will gain you higher marks.

Production choices

Audio and audio-visual (may be collaborative, group production).

You must not produce anything linked to the examination topic!

- **Documentary:** an extract of approximately 3 minutes, an opening sequence or, for television documentary only, a title sequence.
- **Television or radio drama**: a 3-minute extract, an opening sequence, or for television drama only, a title sequence for a new drama for a younger audience.
- **News programme:** an extract of 3 minutes or title sequence and introduction for a news programme targeted at younger audiences.
- **Advert:** two adverts of approximately 30 to 45 seconds (if group) or one advert if individual.
- **Animation:** an extract of approximately 45 seconds to 1 minute.
- **Trailer for film or television programme**: a trailer of approximately 1 minute for a newly devised genre film or television programme.
- **Film**: an extract from a genre film or a complete short film of approximately 3 minutes, an opening sequence or title sequence.
- **Music video:** a 3-minute music video.

Key Term

Clearly defined roles
This means that everyone in the group must have a technical job to do, for example filming, editing or sound. The roles can be shared, for example two people could each do some of the filming and some of the editing, but it must be clear what each person's contribution to the production has been.

Tip

Try not to be too ambitious. Some of the best pieces of work are completed by students who keep their ideas small and manageable.

Print-based options (individual)

- **Comic:** a cover plus one other page or a double-page spread for a younger or adult market.
- **Newspaper**: a front page plus one other page or a double-page spread from a popular, tabloid newspaper; a front page from a 'broadsheet' newspaper.
- **Magazine**: a front cover plus one other page or a double-page spread for the youth audience.
- **Posters**: at least two posters from a marketing campaign for either a new genre film or a television programme or music performers.
- **CD/DVD**: the front and back cover plus spine plus at least one page of an insert for the first CD of a new performer or band.
- **Photostory**: a double-page spread for a magazine targeted at a younger audience.

Interactive media (individual)

- **Website**: a home page plus one linked page.
- **Computer game**: an extract of two scenes from a computer game.
- **Digital story**: a digital story of approximately two minutes.
- **News, entertainment, sports or music package**: one window plus one linked window.
- **Podcast**: a podcast of approximately two minutes.
- **Multimedia slide show**: a series of linked windows with music and voice-over of approximately two minutes.

> **Tip**
>
> Just like with an audio-visual production, try to be creative. Think about what you can do to make your print product a bit different from existing products.

> **Tip**
>
> For print options you must take and use your own images. Make sure that you think about the composition of your photograph carefully. It is much better to start with a good image than try to sort out your mistakes afterwards on a program like Photoshop. This takes up time which could be used being creative with the software.

Examples of print production texts

Commentary

These two examples of magazine front covers successfully show both technical and creative skills. There is clear evidence that the students have researched existing products and used the research to help them to create effective products.

The original images are strong and suit the genre of the magazine. It is clear that the producers of the magazines have instructed their 'models' on what to wear, their expressions and gestures. This is very important if the front cover is to look convincing. Having someone on the front of a fashion magazine in their school uniform will not work!

Layout and design has been well thought out in both texts in order to attract the audience. All of the text can be read and the placing of words and phrases on angles and in differing sizes is effective and eye-catching for the reader. It is clear that the students are confident in using the chosen software.

The use of different font styles and creative layout and design make the pages visually very strong and this is a selling point of the magazines.

Both covers show an understanding of the codes and conventions of this type of magazine.

Examples of audio-visual production texts

A film trailer

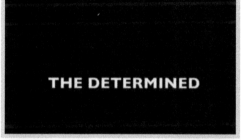

THE DETERMINED

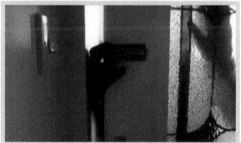

COMING SOON
DECEMBER 17

Commentary

Here you can see stills from a trailer for a horror film. Earlier in this section you will have seen the audience research and recce planning for this. From the selection of images you can see that there is a clear narrative involving a girl leaving home, being chased, returning home thinking she is safe and then we are left with an enigma.

The student demonstrates the codes and conventions of a trailer and of the film's genre. There is also evidence that they have engaged the audience.

Technically, the piece is well structured and you can see, even from these few stills, that there is a range of interesting shots including close-ups and long shots to establish the action. The editing has been well thought out and the pace increased.

Tip

The audio for this trailer was dramatic music and sound effects. Choosing the right music to accompany your moving images is very important. Where you can, avoid lots of dialogue as this can be hard to make realistic.

A fragrance advertisement

Commentary

These are shots from an audio-visual advertisement for a fragrance. The research and planning can be seen earlier in this section. If you look back to the student's research into the *Daisy* fragrance you can clearly see how the findings have been used to influence the style of this campaign.

The locations used in this advert are the ones pictured in the planning recce earlier, showing the importance of thinking of locations that best match the text you want to produce.

Technical competence is shown in the way in which the advert is filmed as if it is on old cine film so giving an old-fashioned, nostalgic feel. Some of the shots are in black and white and a flickering effect has been added in the post-production editing. This is an additional technical skill.

The codes and conventions of an advert of this style have been used and the use of young girls suggests the target audience. The image of the fragrance bottle appears at the end of the advert; this is another typical convention of a fragrance advert.

The only audio code was music, a slow, soft rock style song sung by a female, this suggested the audience and matched the dreamy style of the advert. This decision reflected the audience research shown earlier where the results said that people liked the combination of images, photographs and music.

Key Term

Representations
For example, if you have created a CD cover and insert for a new artist or band, have you considered how to represent them and their style of music through, for example, the use of images, name of the band, font styles, etc.

Tip

Planning out your time to ensure that you meet the deadline set by your teacher is very important.

Evaluation (10 marks)

The following areas need to be explained

- Have you met your aims and purposes?
- How have you used the appropriate codes and conventions of your chosen texts? For example, does your lifestyle magazine front cover look like similar existing products?
- Have you used **representations**?
- How have you used narrative (where appropriate)?
- How have you organised the work to appeal to and engage the audience/user?
- What organisational issues are raised by the text? For example, how your film may be marketed and distributed.

Tip

In your evaluation your viewpoints should be clearly expressed. When you are making media productions, which could include short films, advertisements, newspapers, magazines or web pages, being as creative as possible should be encouraged.

A Class Work Log like this can help you to plan out your time and divide up responsibilities:

Date	Work completed	Targets for next lesson

Success criteria

Research and planning (20 marks)

To gain a Level 3 you must:

- Present evidence relating to textual organisation, e.g. genre, narrative, representation.
- Show an understanding of audiences/users.
- Demonstrate that you have explored other similar examples.
- Use appropriate media terminology.

To gain a Level 4 you must:

- Present your findings in an excellent way showing their relevance to the production in terms of narrative, representation and genre.
- Show a sophisticated understanding of audiences/users and organisations.
- Demonstrate that you have explored other similar examples in detail, making perceptive points.
- Demonstrate an excellent ability to use appropriate media terminology.

Production (50 marks)

To gain a Level 3 you must:

- Use the codes and conventions of the chosen text creatively for your own purposes.
- Edit your production in an appropriate manner.
- Use techniques to encourage audiences to engage with your product.

To gain a Level 4 you must:

- Show an excellent ability to use the codes and conventions of the chosen text **creatively** for your own purposes.
- Engage audiences/users through a range of techniques.
- Show an excellent ability to control the narrative or the audio-visual organisation of the production.
- Demonstrate high production values whatever the technology used in creating the product.

Evaluation (10 marks)

To gain a Level 3 you must:

- Evaluate the typical codes and conventions used in the production.
- Show simple awareness of the audience.
- Communicate using appropriate terminology related to the production.

To gain a Level 4 you must:

- Show an excellent ability to evaluate the typical codes and conventions used in the production.
- Communicate in a developed manner about the issues which arise when your production is distributed.

> **Tip**
> Look closely at what extra things you need to do to move from Level 3 to Level 4. Think about how you can show this in your production work.

PRODUCTION PLANNING SHEET

TOPIC AREA ....

RESEARCH UNDERTAKEN

1. ....

2. ....

3. ....

4. ....

Possible examples of research:
- Annotation of texts
- Devising and conducting surveys and questionnaires
- Focus groups
- Industry research
- Blogs
- Electronic research

PLANNING STAGES

1. ....

2. ....

3. ....

4. ....

Examples may include:
- Scripts
- Character profiles
- Flow charts
- Shot lists/ running orders
- Mood boards
- Designs for sets, costumes, etc.
- Storyboards
- Print mock-ups

PRODUCTION PIECES

2 pages of print or digital media or 3 minutes of audio-visual work.

Briefly outline your ideas for your production pieces below:

....

....

....

....

....

....

....

STORYBOARD

Shot Duration	Visuals	Camera Instructions Shots, angles, movement, transitions	Audio Dialogue, music, SFX	Comment Intended effect on audience

11: Approaching Textual Investigations

Key Terms

Controlled Assessment
This is the work that you do in class that then counts towards your final GCSE grade. The assessments are 'controlled' in that you must complete them in class time under your teacher's supervision. They are also controlled by WJEC, the awarding body, as they set the titles from which you must choose.

Illustrated essay
This is a written piece of work that includes images. For example, if the topic of your investigation is genre conventions in film trailers, you may include some screen shots from your examples to make your point clearer.

Challenged
In this question the expectation is that you will be investigating a media text that shows a different representation or set of genre conventions from the usual ones. For example, a music video that shows a more realistic example of a young woman or an example of narrative that is not a simple linear structure.

Textual investigations are part of the **Controlled Assessment** element of your GCSE course. You must include two Textual investigations in your final assessment file, although you may do more over the course and then choose your two best pieces. The Textual investigations are worth 20 marks each. Usually you will complete these at the end of a topic. They must have a focus of genre, narrative or representation. These are the rules you must follow in completing Textual investigations:

- One must be print based.
- Neither Textual investigation can be based on the topic you have chosen for production.
- One Textual investigation may be based on the examination topic, for example Television Crime Drama.
- The two investigations must be on different topics and media forms.
- One Textual investigation must be based on genre.
- One must be based on narrative or representation.
- In your investigation you should refer to one main text but refer to examples of other texts.
- Your investigation must be between 400 and 850 words.
- Your texts can be chosen by your teacher but the titles are set by the awarding body and you must use one of these.

You can present your Textual investigations as an essay, an **illustrated essay** or a PowerPoint presentation. You can also use annotations.

Textual investigation titles

Genre

- You must include a Textual investigation focused on genre in your assessment file. You must choose one of these titles:
- Investigate how genre conventions are used in (your chosen texts).
- Investigate how far genre conventions are **challenged** in (your chosen texts).
- Investigate how far (your chosen texts) conform to genre conventions.

Narrative

- Explore how narrative is constructed in (your chosen texts).
- Explore the structure of narrative in (your chosen texts).
- Explore how conventional the narrative construction or structure is in (your chosen texts).
- Explore how far the narrative construction or structure in (your chosen texts) challenges conventional narratives.

Representation

- Explore how gender, ethnicity, age, nation, place, events or issues are represented in (your chosen texts).
- Explore how far the representation of one of the following is challenged in (your chosen text): gender, ethnicity, age, nation, place, events or issues.
- Explore how far the representation of one of the following reinforces **conventional points of view** in (your chosen texts): gender, ethnicity, age, nation, place, events or issues.

> ### Key Term
>
> **Conventional points of view** This means that the representation in the text is what is expected by an audience. For example, the representation of the woman in horror films is as a victim.

Tips for completing your Textual investigation

- Choose texts that give you enough to write about. The suggestion is that you have one main text and refer to others in your investigation. However, some texts may be shorter or have less to say about them, for example some print advertisements, so you may need to refer to more texts.
- Show your media knowledge of the topic area. It should be clear to the moderator that you have sat in a Media Studies lesson!
- Use media terminology. This means including vocabulary linked to the texts you are investigating, for example magazine covers.
- If you are investigating longer texts, for example television programmes, you cannot discuss the whole programme in the word allocation. You must select key scenes to discuss that best show what you want to say about the text. You may just want to concentrate your investigation on the opening sequence and another key scene, for example.
- If you are having trouble staying within the word limit, annotating an image instead of writing a paragraph about it will cut down how many words you use.
- Plan your work before you start writing. Complete a rough draft and ask your teacher for some feedback before you hand in your final piece of work.

Success criteria

The success criteria below show what you must do to gain your marks. It is linked to Textual investigations with narrative as the focus.

Lower Level 3

- You have explored narrative conventions in your chosen texts.
- You have shown some awareness of the ways in which an audience can be attracted to a text because of the way in which the narrative is constructed.
- You have focused on one main text but have referred to at least one other.
- You have used some media terminology in your investigation.
- You have organised your investigation and shown your understanding of narrative.

Lower Level 4

- You have shown an excellent ability to explore the narrative structure of your chosen texts.
- Your work is well organised. You have focused on one main text but have referred to other examples.
- You have shown an awareness of both the audience and the organisations that produce the text.
- You have confidently used a wide range of media terms in your investigation.
- You have shown that you clearly understand narrative.
- Your writing and presentation are coherent and very accurate.

Textual investigation examples

Here you will see sections from the Textual investigations of four students who were investigating the following question:

Explore how narrative is constructed in *Vera* and *CSI: Miami*

The students chose one of the texts as their main focus and used the second text as a comparison.

Hazem's introduction:

❶ In this Textual investigation, I will be discussing how narrative is constructed in CSI: Miami and Vera. Narrative is the way in which a text is structured. There are various devices used to keep the attention of the audience. Narratives can be linear or non-linear. ❷ Non-linear narratives include the manipulation of time and space, e.g. flashbacks and slow motion as in CSI: Miami; this is used to attract the attention of the audience who are mostly Americans.

❸ British crime dramas tend to be more conventional and often use a linear format. This is because, in America, there are more channels to compete with, whereas in Britain, audiences tend to channel hop less, therefore Vera is free to be a more down to earth and traditional crime drama. ❹

Commentary

❶ It is useful in an introduction to say which texts you will be exploring in your investigation. It is also important to show, as this candidate has done, that you understand the media concept you are investigating. Don't just jump straight into talking about your texts.

❷ This candidate has used media terminology linked to narrative structure. This shows that he understands the focus of his investigation. He could have explored 'construction' generally here as it is a word from the investigation title. He also starts to link narrative appeal to audience – this can be followed up later.

❸ The candidate has chosen a British and an American example of a crime drama. Choosing two different examples rather than two similar ones means you will usually have different things to say about your texts and will avoid repeating yourself. Choosing a British and American example also means the candidate could discuss organisations and different audiences. He begins to do this here but it is not fully developed.

❹ The candidate starts to explore the differences between the two examples and suggests that this is linked to their structure and that *Vera* is more conventional.

Summative comments

This is a good example of an introduction in which the candidate introduces his texts, the focus of his investigation and starts to think about the differences between *CSI: Miami* and *Vera*.

Yasamin: Understanding of the focus of the question

Commentary

In this extract from a candidate's work, she shows her understanding of narrative.

❶ Yasamin has introduced an important theory related to narrative and has explained it briefly. She has avoided falling into the trap of spending too long explaining the theory as she would waste words.

❷ She applies the theory to her text but also shows how it is a bit different by referring to 'flexi-narratives'.

❸ Here she says how the narrative structure has an effect on the audience. This is one of the points in the success criteria. She also includes a specific example from her text to show she has studied a particular episode from the series.

❹ She makes a comparison with her second text and includes more media terminology linked to narrative. She again shows how the structure, using an enigma, can affect an audience.

❺ Here she shows how technical codes are part of the narrative and have an effect on an audience. Backing this point up with an example would have helped here.

Summative comments

This paragraph is well structured and uses a range of media terminology linked to the investigation focus of narrative. There is also some use of specific examples from the chosen texts. Yasamin could have included more of these to make her points clear.

Typically, crime dramas have a linear narrative according to **❶** Todorov's theory; all events happen in chronological order and there is no manipulation in time. **❷** Vera is linear in structure; however, there are also flexi-narratives making it more complex. **❸** This gives the audience of Vera a better view of the characters' lives outside of their job; for instance, by introducing Joe's past with Robert Doran it helps the audience to get to know him better than as just a police officer. On the other hand, in CSI: Miami, the audience only have very faint knowledge of the characters' lives. Instead, flashbacks are used, some of which are misleading to add to the enigma of the story as well as to get the audience more involved. **❹** In building the music up to a crescendo in CSI: Miami, the tension and excitement increases within the audience. **❺**

Will: Investigating characters

❶ Vera as a character is, like I said, much more conventional when it comes to crime drama and also when it comes to the sub-genre of British crime drama. She is devoted to her work, which causes her to be very lonely and she works very carefully and explores every option, ❷ You can compare this type of character with British crime dramas of the past such as Inspector Morse ❸ Vera and her work partner Joe are binary opposites. ❹ When we look at Horatio of CSI:Miami, he is typical of an American crime drama, he gets straight to the point and when he discovers something new, the scene changes and we are straight there and something new happens. ❺

Commentary

❶ In this paragraph from a Textual investigation the candidate focuses on character and their role in the narrative.

❷ These are good points; an example from the episode would have made them clearer.

❸ By referring to an example of an older crime drama with a strong character, the candidate shows his wider understanding of the topic.

❹ The candidate uses media terminology to show how the characters in the crime drama work together. He could have said more about how Joe's character is different from Vera and how they may appeal to different audiences.

❺ The candidate makes a good, brief reference to another text and character. He begins to show an understanding about organisations.

Summative comments

This paragraph has a clear focus that is linked to an aspect of narrative. There is good use of general examples; more specific ones would have shown more detailed understanding. There is a clear awareness of how some characters are typical of the sub-genre. He could have used some annotated images to make his points clearer.

Rachel: Investigating technical codes

Commentary

Here, the focus of the paragraph is technical codes and how they affect the narrative.

❶ The candidate is clear about the effect of technical codes upon the audience. There is also reference to a particular scene; this could have been explained more fully to make the point clearer.

❷ The candidate uses sophisticated media terminology related to narrative and links it to an example.

❸ Here the candidate uses an example and refers to a camera shot and angle showing the effect they have on the audience. She makes a sophisticated point linking the lighting to the narrative 'we are in the dark'. We can't see and we don't understand what is happening.

❹ Here the candidate includes another example of a shot. The candidate could have taken a screen shot of this example and included it in her essay with some annotation to make her point clear.

Summative comments

This is a very good paragraph showing the candidate's understanding of how technical codes can help the narrative. The fact that this paragraph has a clear focus shows her investigation is well organised. There is very good use of media terminology and a real sense that this candidate knows what she is talking about. Use of images to illustrate her points would have helped.

In Vera, in the scene of the shooting, the technical codes constantly change our point of view, which helps the audience feel as if they are included in the narrative. ❶ The scene also includes privileged spectator position so we have a better knowledge of the killer than the characters in the programme and this makes us watch on. ❷ The scene in the interview room includes a dark setting and low angle and over the shoulder shots to make you feel you are in the room with them. The dark setting gives the impression that we are in the dark, with only natural lighting which makes it more realistic. ❸ The high angle camera shot in the last scene of Vera shows her vulnerability as the house is a lot bigger than her. ❹

12: Examination Practice and Technique

The GCSE examination will be at the end of your GCSE course. It counts towards 40% of your final GCSE grade. It will be focused on a topic set by the awarding body (WJEC). You will be told the topic and you will prepare for the examination during the course. It may be that one of your Textual investigations will be based on the examination topic. Section 4 of this guide explains the structure of the examination paper. The examination paper is 2 hours 15 minutes long and is split into two sections:

Section A: Thinking about the Media: Investigating

Section B: Thinking about the Media: Planning

Section A

In this part of the examination you will be shown some material linked to the set topic; for example, in 2014 this may be an extract related to television crime drama. This section is worth 40 marks.

What can I do to prepare?

- Practise making notes. This is not something you will be able to do automatically; making useful notes that help you to answer the questions is a skill that must be learned. If the extract for Section A is audio-visual, you will be expected to make notes while you are watching. If you are given a print text as stimulus you still need to make some notes before you start to write your response. Grids using headings are good ways to get down your thoughts and ideas and to pick out examples from the text you are given to investigate.

- Revise your key media terminology. Know what you are expected to write about. Remember, the question will not give you the media terminology, you will be expected to use it in your answer. For example, if you are asked to identify sounds in an audio-visual extract you will need to be aware of the different audio codes you could mention and the correct vocabulary to describe them:

Tip

Read the question carefully. Be clear about what you are expected to write about. For Section A, the questions will give you a focus for your note-taking, you will not need to make notes on everything in the extract, you will need to be selective.

Tip

Understanding the structure of the examination paper and the marks awarded for questions will help you to prepare and know what to expect.

- Sound effects
- Music
- Dialogue
- Diegetic and non-diegetic sound.

Key Terms

Identify
This means 'pick out' or 'find an example of'. For example: *Identify two camera shots in this opening sequence.*

Explain
Here you will be expected to explore what you have selected in more detail; for example, explaining how and why the camera shots you have chosen have been used.

- Be clear about the focus of the different questions in Section A. Questions 1 and 2 will be linked to the stimulus material and may ask you to **identify** and **explain**. These questions will ask you to explore the stimulus material and may cover:
  - Camera shots
  - Iconography and settings
  - Genre, narrative and characters
  - Use of colour
  - Graphics/font style
  - Visual codes: clothing, gesture, expression
  - Other aspects of the design and layout for a print text.

- For questions 3 and 4 you need to be prepared to explore broader areas of the Media Studies Framework, for example organisations and audience. Revisit Section 2 of this guide to revise what makes up the framework. These questions tend to be worth more marks so you need to make sure that you have enough to say in your response. It will help if you have practised answering some questions like this under timed conditions at home or in the classroom. The questions may cover:

Representation

- How age, gender, ethnicity, nation or cultural diversity are represented in this type of text.
- How the representations within the text are constructed, for example through technical codes.
- Whose ideas are contained within the text?
- Are the representations stereotypical?

Narrative

- How narratives are structured to create meaning.

Audience

- The appeal of the text, how the text targets audiences, why the text is popular with audiences, for example.

Organisations

- The promotion and marketing of media texts.
- How the industry is regulated and controlled.
- The importance of the texts for their industry.

- For questions 3 and 4 you will be expected to include some specific examples from the set topic, for example television crime dramas (2014) or print advertisements (2015). You need to use examples that are different from the

Tip
Use the glossary at the back of this guide to help you to improve your technical vocabulary.

resource used in the examination. You will have looked at some examples in class but, as part of your examination preparation, make sure that you have also spent some time independently researching other examples. Think of a way in which you can keep a record of the examples you have watched or looked at so that you remember them when you come to revise. A grid like this may help you:

Example	Aspects of the text: Genre /narrative	Areas of representation	Audience	Marketing / promotion
Information: Channel Producers Agency				

- Revise the media theories you have learned, for example uses and gratifications for an audience question. Including relevant theories will help you to produce a more sophisticated response and to show your broad understanding of the media and your topic.

Section B

This section tests your planning and creative skills and your knowledge of the examination topic. It will also test your ability to explain the creative decisions you have made. In this section you will not be shown any examples, instead you will be asked to plan and create ideas of your own for a new text. This section is worth 40 marks. Be sure that you understand what you are going to be required to do in this section of the examination paper. Because you know what the topic will be, for example Television Magazines linked to the overall topic of TV Drama in 2014, or Television Advertising for 2015, you can do quite a lot of planning in advance.

Make sure that you understand the codes and conventions of the text you may be asked to create. Practise designing different types of texts related to the topic, for example a front cover of a listings magazine featuring a new crime drama or a double-page feature spread about the new crime drama. Although you will have planned some ideas in advance of the examination, make sure that you read the tasks carefully and be prepared to adapt your ideas. For example, if the task asks you to design your text for a particular target audience.

A planning grid like the one on page 139 will help you to set out your ideas.

The examination is not a test of your artistic skills but the expectation is that you will be able to show that you understand what is required in, for example, a storyboard or a magazine cover. Do not worry if your text does not look exactly like you want it to as you may be asked to **annotate** your design and in one of the tasks, to **justify** your decisions.

Key Terms

Annotate
This means labelling your design to show that you understand the main codes and conventions. This is also your chance to quickly show that you can use the correct media terms.

Justify
This means explain why you included what you have in your text. For example, why you have used that shot in the storyboard for a television advert. You will also need to say how what you have created will attract an audience.

Tip

You can change the headings of the grid to suit the topic you are studying.

Tip

Revisit Section 2: Media Studies Framework to remind yourself of audience theories, then think about how you can apply them to your examination topic.

QUICKFIRE
62

If you were labelling a magazine cover you had created, what key terms would you use?

The last task in this section is broader and is related to the text you have created. For example, it may ask you to explain why television advertising is important to the makers of products or explain the techniques they use to appeal to the target audience. This means that you must make sure that you understand the industry that produces texts like the one you have created. You can use specific examples of texts to help you to make your points. Make sure that you have thought about some actual examples before you go into the examination.

Summary: dos and don'ts for examination preparation

- DO – Look at some **past papers**. They will not focus on the same topic as the one you will be studying, BUT the structure and types of questions will be similar.
- DO – Learn the media terms related to your topic area.
- DO – Look at some examples of texts from your topic in addition to the ones you have studied in class.
- DO – Keep a record of the examples you have looked at inside and outside of lessons.
- DO – Practise answering exam-type questions under timed conditions.
- DO – Plan some ideas for Section B before you go into the examination BUT be prepared to adapt them if you need to.
- DON'T – Describe, try to analyse the texts in Section A.
- DON'T – Think you will have time to think up your ideas in the exam! You won't.
- DON'T – Spend too long on the creative task, for example colouring in the storyboard – it isn't an Art examination! If you have time at the end, you can come back to it.

Why is it important to plan for Section B in advance?

GCSE Media Studies: examination responses

Below are some responses to the questions set In the Summer 2013 examination. The topic was Television Drama. The focus of Section A was Television Drama (excluding crime) and Section B was Web-based Drama. Each year the examination focus will be different but these responses and the commentary will help you to see how and where marks can be picked up.

Please note: The general points about responses can transfer to all topics but don't memorise these questions and answers because they won't be in your exam paper!

Section A

The candidates were shown an extract from ITV's TV drama *Downton Abbey.*

1 (a) Identify **two** different settings used in the extract. [4]

(b) Briefly explain why these **two** settings are used. [6]

Tom's answer

1(a) 1. A warzone, such as the battlefield or trenches.
2. Home, such as the dining room and the bedroom.

1(b) Explanation 1: The warzone gives a faster-paced ❶ action scene, thus appealing to the younger audience ❷. The fact that they showed the inside feel of a war makes it seem realistic; this also will draw audience members in as they will believe they are a part of it. The younger audience tends to like fast paced action ❷; a war is a place for a lot of action making the show start with audience members on the edge of their seats. ❸

Explanation 2: A home is used to calm the tone. It calms the tone so that the audience will know what is happening in the characters' lives. ❹ The war made it harder to listen due to background noise but in the home it was more clear ❺. Home is where general issues take place, ❻ so this brings in a wider range of audience members appealing to war fighters and to the everyday people as there are scenes relating to both.

Examiner commentary

Q1 (a). There were a range of settings to choose from between the battlefields and the inside and outside of the country house. This candidate has chosen two different examples and has picked up the four marks by backing up the general setting with a specific example.

Q1 (b). The important word in this question is **'why'**. This means that you must develop what you have said in the first question and **explain** the purpose and effect of the settings. Here the candidate explains the settings they have chosen. In Explanation 1 they refer to the pace of the extract ❶ and they also suggest how this appeals to an audience ❷. They develop this point by suggesting that this is part of the structure of the programme intending to 'hook' the audience from the start. You will notice that they do repeat the same point; you need to make sure that you make a range of different points in order to pick up marks and show your understanding. They also add another 'why' point related to making the programme more realistic. ❸

In Explanation 2 the candidate again relates the setting to the effect on the audience ❹ and makes some reference to the audio used ❺. There is also some suggestion that this setting may create a different narrative. ❻

To improve the response the candidate could have mentioned:

- How technical codes, for example camera shots, movement and angles, helped to create the setting.

- How iconography, for example clothing and props, added to the setting.

- The sub-genre of the TV Drama: Period/Costume Drama and how the setting showed the genre's codes and conventions.

- How the setting linked to the possible narratives. This was mentioned briefly but not developed.

131

2 (a) Identify **two** different storylines in the extract. [4]

   (b) Briefly explain how **each** of the storylines appeals to an audience. [6]

Examiner commentary

Notice that certain words are in bold. This means that the examiner wants you to make sure you follow the instructions!

(a) The two examples of narratives are similar and not fully developed.

(b) The word 'storylines' is used in the question but the expectation is that you will be able to use the media term 'narrative'.

Explanation 1 shows a confident explanation of the appeal of the storyline to a specific audience ❶. The candidate attempts to link the narrative of the Period Drama to a modern audience and suggests the effect of the drama on the audience ❷. There is also a relevant point about how the narrative structure manipulates the audience ❸. However, there is very limited use of media language and a lack of understanding of the codes and conventions of the narrative of this sub-genre. The expectation is that the candidate may have discussed characters, plot situations and narrative techniques to develop the answer.

Explanation 2: This response is less secure as the Television Drama is based around the First World War therefore an audience may not relate directly to the events. ❹ The same point is made again ❺, the candidate needed to develop the answer by including, as above, references to the characters, dialogue, technical codes, etc. There is an understanding that there is a development in the story that changes the feel of the scene ❻, this is relevant but needed to be discussed in more detail to gain more marks and to show understanding.

To improve the above response the candidate could have mentioned:

- The specific role of the characters in the narrative.

- The audience expectations of narratives in this sub-genre.

- How technical codes show the narrative.

- Narrative theory, for example Todorov/Propp, and how themes like conflict develop the narrative.

- What appeals this sub-genre has for an audience, for example insight into different worlds and the class system of the time.

- Narrative techniques that are used to appeal to the audience, for example enigmas.

Tom's answer

2(a) 1. The life of a war fighter.
2. The life of an achieved war fighter who is now a father.

2(b) Explanation 1: The war fighter lifestyle appeals to the audience that closely relate ❶, e.g. soldiers. It appeals to them as it helps show everyone else how hard these soldiers actually work, risking their lives so our lives are brighter. It helps others sympathise ❷ towards the soldiers and inspires and influences others to join the army to help. This storyline appeals to a variety of audience members through manipulation, ❸ since the warfighter is now highly respected.

Explanation 2: The life of an achieved warfighter appeals to retired people who want to keep their family relations strong. ❸ This appeals to them as it relates to their lifestyle ❹. The fact that the character on the television drama is facing the same issues as the person watching ❺ helps audience members feel like they're not alone. So it appeals to audience members with hope of reassurance. The calm atmosphere helps situations turn more serious as the atmosphere suddenly turns negative. ❻

Rummana's answer

2(a) 1. The soldier in the war, dreaming of Downton.
2. The mystery of why Sybil is crying, who is it about?

2(b) Explanation 1: This storyline appeals to the audience because it makes them feel sympathy for the protagonist as he battles for survival emphasising how real the situation is for him. The protagonist acts like a hero in Propp's theory, saving a fellow soldier thus increasing the audience's love for this character. Furthermore, during the battlefield scene the lighting remains dark and gloomy symbolising death, but as soon as he mentions 'Downton' the lighting shines upon his face emphasising his positive emotion thus making the audience feel relieved and pleased for this character and they want to go further into the programme to see if he does return to Downton.

Explanation 2: This second storyline creates audience appeal by leaving the clip with a cliffhanger, who is that letter from? who is it about? thus appealing to the audience increasing their desire into the programme, watching it further to answer these questions. In addition the crying Sybil causes the audience to feel sympathy for her, it could be the loss of a lover, family friend, something everyone has, causing the audience to relate and think what would I do if I lost my sister, lover, etc. This then increases the audience's relationship with the cast. Furthermore the target audience for the genre is females and with this storyline females do sympathise and get more emotional easily with these storylines. The producers have appealed to their target audience through their storylines.

Examiner commentary

Rummana's response is more detailed and sophisticated. She uses a range of media terminology and is aware of the effect of the narrative on an audience. Notice how, when we read it, we can see that she has watched and understood the extract and uses it to help her to understand the question.

TASK

1. Look again at the bullet pointed list on page 132. Find examples of when Rummana makes these points in her answer to question 2 (b).

2. Summarise briefly how she has answered the question well.

3. This is a sophisticated answer – what more could she have done to make her response 'outstanding'?

3. Explain how age is represented in **one** Television Drama you have studied. [10]

Examiner commentary

This is an example of a confident response.

The candidate has chosen a relevant example of a TV Drama ❶ and one that offers opportunities to write about the representation of age. He also develops the idea to include class and authority and the fact that this affects the narrative and the way in which characters respond to each other in the programme ❷. This is a good point and the candidate develops this further to discuss age and experience ❸. A specific example from an episode of *Waterloo Road* would have helped to make the point clearer.

The candidate makes a general point about how an audience may view the behaviour of young people in comparison to older people. The candidate tends to stay with the same point. As there is not much time to complete each question, it is important to make as many different points as possible ❹.

The candidate does move on to begin to discuss stereotyping in this TV Drama and so shows his ability to use media terminology and his understanding of representation ❺.

There is a reference to a specific narrative situation in the programme and this links to the candidate's earlier points about age and what is expected of adults and their behaviour ❻.

In this last paragraph the candidate makes a point about how the representations in this TV Drama reflect real life although this is not very clearly communicated. This final paragraph is also a conclusion to the answer and gives the whole response a structure ❼.

To improve the above response the candidate could have mentioned:

- A greater range of specific examples of age from the episode of *Waterloo Road* studied including reference to specific characters and/or storylines.

- Reference to how representations are constructed through, for example, clothing, expression, gesture, dialogue, narrative.
  - The link between the representations and different audience responses.

Tom's answer

Below are extracts from the response:

A Television Drama I studied is Waterloo Road ❶. In this drama, the age of somebody represents their class (superior or inferior). The fact that students are younger than the teacher gives the teacher an advantage over them. The teacher, being the authoritative figure, has the final say in arguments as his age gives him an upper hand ❷. Age shows experience, so this experience is what makes students respect and listen to their teacher as their teacher has been through more. More experience a person has, the wiser they will be as people don't usually tend to make second mistakes ❸. The fact that the students are of a young age makes it seem as if their behaviour is excusable. The naïve mistakes are what will make them grow, so many mistakes are tolerated ❹.

Age may help the students get away with the mistakes but it also gives students restrictions. Their age is what limits them from crossing the line as there will be consequences.

The fact that students tend to solve situations through fights makes it seem as if all students do it. A majority of problems went violent in Waterloo Road. This gives a natural yet stereotypical view of the lives of students ❺.

The fact that if a teacher makes a mistake and gets fired shows a more mature view. The age of these people making mistakes has more serious consequences. This represents age as a factor of no restrictions ❻.

The representations of age in Waterloo Road give a clearer understanding of the modern society through uses of its overused scenes, the problems you get into and showing the differences of resolving these issues as a teacher and a student ❼.

4. Explain why Television Drama continues to be popular with television audiences.

[10]

Joe's answer

TV Drama dominates TV scheduling and is often on at primetime because it reaches some of the channels' highest viewing figures by appealing to a mass audience ❶ through TV Drama's many sub-genres such as teen drama and period drama ❷. TV Drama is popular with audiences as it tackles contemporary and relevant issues that the audience will be able to relate to and identify with their own lives ❸, which makes it accessible viewing for a broad range of people. This is reinforced by the domestic settings used to make a synergy between the lives of the characters in the drama and the audience's lives so they can feel more engaged with the narratives. ❹

They also include dramatic multi-stranded narratives with intriguing narratives causing audience curiosity. Also they can conform to Todorov's narrative structure by creating disruption and heartbreak but also creating a new equilibrium, which gives the audience satisfaction as they feel justice has been done and the good overcame the evil. ❺

They use domestic settings and make them iconic such as The Rovers Return pub in Coronation Street, which makes the settings recognisable for the audience, which makes them feel more involved and reassured as they are familiar with the location ❻.

Examiner commentary

This is an excellent response to Question 4.

The candidate immediately shows his understanding of organisations by referring to the scheduling and the importance of TV Dramas to channels ❶. There is also an understanding that TV Drama as a genre can be split into sub-genres which hold different appeals for audiences ❷.

The candidate also begins to discuss the relationship between the TV Drama and the audience and why people watch them. He could have referred to the uses and gratifications theory here and shown his ability to use relevant media terminology and a sophisticated theory ❸.

The candidate makes a new, relevant point about settings and how they can make the audience feel involved. An example from a TV Drama would have helped to make the point clear. ❹

The candidate then moves on to refer to the role of the narrative in attracting an audience. Here he shows an excellent understanding of terminology related to narrative and theory. He also links this back to the effect on the audience, in this way he stays focused on the question. He touches on binary opposites in his discussion of good and evil. This is a very secure paragraph but would have been improved with a specific example from a TV Drama ❺.

The candidate returns to the point about settings but this paragraph is stronger as it includes a specific example, although this could have been developed in greater detail. Again, he successfully links the setting to the audience ❻.

To improve the above response the candidate could have mentioned:

- More specific examples from TV Dramas he had studied in class to show his broad knowledge.

- The production values of the TV Drama.

- The various forms, for example two-parters, 'one-offs', series.

- Other codes and conventions, for example characters, with specific examples.

Examiner commentary

You will not be set the same tasks as this, your Section B topic will be different but, like this candidate, you will have to use the creative tasks in this section to show your understanding of the topic area and your ability to evaluate what you have created.

Emily shows her understanding of the web-based form by deciding to create a spin-off. This means that she can make good points about audience recognition and expectation and the fact that web-based dramas tend to have a young audience. She has thought about how to appeal to this target audience. ❶

In her choice of characters she shows her understanding of the conventions of the vampire genre, she has chosen a genre she is confident with. ❷

Her explanations clearly discuss the role of each of the characters. She explains how they will attract the teenage audience and uses media terminology related to representation ❸.

She also shows some creativity in the second character by making him a bit different. She then explains how an audience may respond to this character ❹. She also shows her understanding of the conventions of the genre ❺.

To improve the above response the candidate could have mentioned:

More of the conventions of the form – the web-based drama. There is no indication in the explanation that this is not a more traditional TV Drama, apart from the focus of the younger audience.

Section B

Here are extracts from one candidate's responses to the creative Section B questions from summer 2013.

5. You work for a television company that wants to develop a new web-based drama.

Task 1

Choose a name for your web-based drama. Briefly explain why you chose this name. [4]

Emily's answer

Name of web-based drama: Playing Human

Brief explanation: ❶ I chose this name because my web-based drama is a spin-off of the popular hit 'Being Human'. And as my target audience involves teenagers and I used 'playing' as an alternative word for 'Being' as 'playing' connotes youth, excitement and fun and I want my audience to relate and be entertained.

Task 2

(a) Suggest two characters for your web-based drama. [2]

(b) Briefly explain each of their roles. [4]

Emily's answer

1. Aidan Turner the stereotypical vampire.

2. Arthur Johnson the counter stereotype werewolf. ❷

Explanation 1: Aidan's role is to initially draw in the female teenage audience with his insanely good looks and fit body mesmerising the primary audience ❸ making them desire to be with him to create obsession with his character. Also because he is a stereotypical vampire he is attractive then draws in his prey and he goes into the kill.

Explanation 2: Arthur's character surprises the audience ❹. His role is to keep the audience on their feet. He has two sides to him, a quite geeky personality when at school but when the iconography of the full moon ❺ comes in he turns vicious. The appeal to the audience is questioning what he is going to do next ❻.

Task 3

Outline the storyline for the first webisode.   [10]

Emily's answer

The storyline for the first webisode is to initially introduce the characters' individual personalities and supernatural features, and then to discuss how and why they are who they are, then towards the end after a minor battle they will become friends ❶.

We get to see the character's personality through their costume, iconography and facial expressions ❷ and the contrast between the supernaturals' normal life and when their violent and animal side comes to the surface. The storyline follows Todorov's theory; it begins with the equilibrium ❸. In this webisode it begins at the first day of school, the setting will be a high school, the generic conventions for the teenage audience ❹ followed by a disruption – a poster advertising a missing girl 'Ana', but the ghost Ana is looking at the poster screaming at it hoping someone will hear her but no one does, causing the audience to feel sympathy towards her ❺. Aidan, the vampire, walks down the corridor, immediate curiosity is shown as he is the only one who can see her and he realises she is dead and Ana is unaware of this, this is the disruption.

The attempts to repair is when the vampire gets his friend Arthur who takes Ana back to his house and they explain who they are and how they became supernatural involving flashbacks turning this into a non-linear episode ❻. At the end of the episode Aidan and Arthur promise that they will find her murderer but Aidan's face looks afraid and guilty, there's something he is not telling. Thus creates audience appeal by engaging them to watch the next episode to find out what happens ❼.

Examiner commentary

In outlining a storyline Emily needed to show creativeness and imagination, an understanding of the codes and conventions of the chosen genre and an idea of how audiences may be attracted to the web drama. She does this by:

❶ Giving an initial overview and stating the aim of the first webisode.

❷ Suggesting how the characters will be created using the conventions of the genre.

❸ Explaining the structure of the storyline and linking this to Todorov's linear structure.

❹ Developing other areas of the narrative including the setting and explaining how her choice of setting will attract a teenage audience.

❺ The introduction of the new character – Ana, fits into the genre but adds interest for the audience and gives further ideas for the narrative to develop. The candidate also suggests how the audience may respond to this character.

❻ Emily introduces narrative techniques showing her understanding and her ability to use media terminology.

❼ The use of the cliffhanger at the end is a creative device and she establishes an enigma.

What could the candidate have added?

More to suggest that this is a web-based drama, not a TV Drama. This may have been through ideas for the length of the webisode, as they are shorter than TV episodes, or by suggesting the use of lower production values, for example unknown actors.

Task 4

Explain how your web-based drama will appeal to audiences. [10]

Examiner commentary

In Section B, whatever topic is set, you may be asked to explain the decisions you have made and how what you have created will appeal to an audience.

For this question the expectation was that the candidate would:

- Have a clear idea of the target audience for their web-based drama.

- Explain how the genre conventions including characters, narrative, representations and technical and audio codes would appeal to the target audience.

- Show awareness of the conventions of a web-based drama and how it is different from more traditional TV Dramas.

- Use media terminology effectively.

Task

Look at Emily's response. Find examples of the bullet points above to show that she has produced a very good explanation.

What could she have done to improve her response?

Emily's answer

My web-based drama appeals to the primary audience of teenagers and a secondary audience of teenage boys. My web-based drama initially appeals to the target audience by the ensemble cast used. Each character has a different personality therefore appealing and relating to a different audience member, thus making it appeal to a wider audience.

Aidan is an attractive, fit teenage boy, the one that every girl wants to be with and the one every boy wants to be, this character attracts the primary audience because they desire to be with him 24/7 and this character also reels in the secondary audience because they can relate to his costume, iconography and his problems, seeing if they would react the same.

Furthermore, Arthur is a stereotype, he is a cute, geeky teenager who is considered a lower status in a high school, but when the full moon appears he turns into a vicious animal. This contrast in personalities leaves the audience wondering who is he, he can't be both surely, also he attracts the secondary audience, teenage boys, because they might be able to relate and also the other teenage boys who like the werewolf character because he is the generic convention of the horror/supernatural genre. Also the ghost Ana creates audience appeal due to her pretty attractive looks by making the primary audience relate to her or desire to be her and the teenage boy audience aspiring to be with her. Also it creates audience appeal because they feel sorry for her.

Section B: TV Listings Magazine Planning

Create a front cover featuring a new crime drama		Explain the reasons for your decisions – how will your cover attract an audience?
Name of magazine		
Target audience of magazine and drama		
Name and sub-genre of new crime drama		
Ideas for central image		
Text to accompany central image		
Ideas for other content to be featured on the front cover, e.g. cover lines		
Other ideas for design elements to show this is a TV listings magazine		

Create a double-page spread for a listings magazine featuring a new crime drama		Explain the reasons for your decisions – how will your ideas attract an audience?
Name of magazine		
Target audience		
Name and sub-genre of new crime drama		
Ideas for layout and design of double-page spread, e.g. pull quotes		
Ideas for headline for page, e.g. may be a pun on the name of the crime drama		
Ideas for images from crime drama to use, e.g. setting, characters, action shot		

Quickfire answers

1 What is the Media?

1 It is important to understand the media and how it works as it is all around us every day and has an influence on our lives, what we think and how we behave.

2 People of different ages consume the media differently sometimes because of what they are used to and have grown up with. Older people may not be as comfortable with new technologies for watching television programmes, for example computers and tablets. Younger people use their mobile phones more often to watch/listen to/read media texts as they are more used to this method.

3 It is important to be aware of how much we are surrounded by the media so that we can think about the effect it may be having on us and do something about it.

4 Older people may not be comfortable with the content of some television programmes because they are not the target audience. They may find the bad language and sexual content of some texts, for example, offensive. However, we must not assume that all old people will think this way.

5 Regulating the Internet is difficult because it is vast and anyone can put on anything they want to. Individuals can regulate which sites can be used; for example, parents can put blocks on home computers. Your school will have blocks in place. Work is also being done to try to make Google and Facebook more responsible for content of their sites.

2 Media Studies Framework

6 The type of setting may be recognisable to an audience because they are used to seeing it, for example the rooms of houses in soap operas. Other settings may give clues to the genre, for example the interview room in a police station will tell audiences that they are watching a police drama.

7 The initial action introduced in the directions is what would be expected in a hospital drama. Also the language used related to the injury and the medication gives clues to the genre.

8 If a character enters a scene in a hospital drama wearing a suit, holding a stethoscope and giving out orders we assume he is a consultant and an audience will have expectations of how the character will behave. Advertisements also use stereotypes as they have less time to communicate messages; the mother/housewife stereotype is used in adverts for cleaning products.

9 All media texts are in competition with other similar texts. If a text, for example a magazine, appeals to its audience, they will buy this instead of another similar magazine and so make money for the magazine's producers.

10 Different industries have different ways of showing that the texts they produce are successful. For a website it will be how many hits it has and for a film it will be box office numbers. Television programmes use ratings to work out which shows are popular.

11 No. Although there is a large group of female gamers it is still the case that boys and men play games more than girls and women.

12 Think about the media texts you watch/read in order to be entertained and to escape from everyday life, for example action films and situation comedies. What about texts you use for information, Internet sites? Social networking sites keep you up to date and you may watch programmes like *Hollyoaks* and *Waterloo Road* for personal identity.

13 An audience may have an oppositional reading of a text if, for example, they have had personal experience of something and then they see it in a TV programme and don't agree with the way it is presented. For example, a nurse may think that the storylines and the behaviour of characters in *Casualty* are very unrealistic.

3 Toolkit for Analysis

14 In your examples think about what the clothing says about the person who wears it and why that might be important in a media text. For example, a woman in a smart suit in a fragrance advert suggests she is modern and powerful. A woman may then buy the fragrance because she wants to be like the woman in the advert.

15 The way the characters are dressed tells us that this film is from the science fiction genre. To add to this there are also images of planets and other objects to do with space. The older characters/actors are bigger and at the top suggesting that they are important. The positioning of the male characters tells us that they may be more important than the female characters. The mode of address of most of the images of the characters is direct suggesting that the film may be dramatic.

16 Extreme close-ups are usually used to show the audience more detail but also to restrict what they can see in order to build tension. For example, an unknown hand slowly turning a door handle in a horror film. The purpose of your example may be one of these. The effect on the audience is that they will be afraid and have expectations of what will happen next.

17 Your examples could have included romantic mood music in a romantic film, dramatic music in the chase scene of a TV drama or sinister, eerie music in a horror film.

18 Airbrushing effects are used by texts to create the idea of perfection. Particularly with advertising, the producers of the products want us to believe that the product had this effect on the person so we will buy it.

4 What is a Topic?

19 In TV, drama may be presented as a regular series, for example *Coronation Street*, on radio it may be presented as a weekly play on Radio 4. The magazine *Radio Times*, presents new or returning dramas on their front covers or features them on the inside pages. Web dramas are a relatively new way of presenting dramas online, for example *E20* which is a spin-off from *EastEnders*.

5 Television Crime Drama

20 Different characters within the team may attract different types of audience. For example, in *New Tricks* there is a strong female character and recognisable older actors who will bring in their own fan base.

21 Schedules are important to advertisers as they allow them to see which programmes appear when and then pick the slot when they think the target audience for their type of product will be watching.

22 Audiences no longer have to rely on the schedules as with technology like BBC iPlayer they can catch up on programmes they have missed when it is convenient for them.

23 Watch again facilities allow audiences to miss out the adverts therefore advertisers will not make any money or sell their products. Recently advertisers have been looking at ways other than television to reach audiences. This means that channels like ITV will lose the money they would make for selling advertising space in their programmes.

24 You would expect to see an idea of setting, clues to the sub-genre and shots of the main characters showing their roles in the narrative.

25 If the sub-genre of the crime drama is forensics, for example, you would expect the settings to include labs and crime scenes. American crime dramas may include more exotic, dramatic settings to hold the attention of the audience.

26 The still of the plot situation from *CSI* shows the team around a table on which there are images from a crime scene. They look as if they are discussing the crime. Behind them is the board with images of victims/suspects, this is a common convention of a crime drama. The older man at the head of the table looks as if he is in charge and is leading the discussion.

27 Fast-paced editing suggests action and involves the audience. Tracking shots following a victim or villain also make the audience feel part of the action as do close-up shots to show emotions like fear or shock.

28 The worlds presented in British crime dramas, for example *Vera*, tend to be more realistic and recognisable. This is helped through technical codes like low key lighting and by using real locations. American crime drama worlds tend to be more dramatic and less realistic. In *CSI: Miami*, for example, the team only ever have one crime to focus on and it is always solved in the end.

6 Advertising and Marketing

29 You may come across an advertisement:
- In a magazine
- In a newspaper
- On the side of a bus
- On a mobile phone
- On a billboard
- On a website
- On a bus shelter
- On a leaflet/flyer.
- On the television/radio/at the cinema

30 If the star chosen to endorse the product is pictured in the press, for example behaving badly, this will reflect badly on the product.

31 Members of the public are usually used to endorse more 'ordinary', everyday products like washing powders and cleaning products. An audience are more likely to believe them than a celebrity.

32 A hard sell print advertisement will usually be clear and to the point. It will often include an image of the product, the price in bold, where you can by it and how much you are saving. Other persuasive techniques will be to tell the audience 'sale ends soon'.

33 Memorable pop songs catch the attention of an audience and they will associate the song with the product. If they like the song they may be more likely to buy the product.

34 The advantage of the Internet is the range of ways in which an advertiser can reach an audience. This can be through search engines, pop ups, pop unders and specifically targeting an audience using information about what they have bought in the past.

35 This model is more useful because it categorises audiences into the types of people they are. This gives an advertiser more information about how they can target different audiences.

36 The use of the England shirt, the British bulldog breed and the Cockney accent are stereotypical characteristics of being English. The sound of bagpipes, the Scottish flag, the hatred of all things English and the strong accent are stereotypical elements of the Scottish nation.

37 This may be because the younger target audience for this product are more easily reached through the Internet and social network sites. They are less likely to view advertisements on the television.

38 The user of a website is offered many more interactive opportunities than a television viewer. They can look at all of the adverts in the campaign, enter competitions, find out about events related to the product and contribute to blogs, etc. This makes them more likely to buy the product.

39 The ideas of the audience are important if the product is to target them successfully. No product would ever be launched without some form of audience research to find out what audiences do and don't like about existing products and what they would want to see in a new product.

7 Lifestyle and Celebrity

40 She is an easily recognisable star who is popular with the target audience for the product. In addition she has very good hair and her regional Geordie accent makes her seem more down to earth and ordinary. People will trust what she says about the product.

41 The celebrity may become unpopular or be in the public eye in a negative way, this would not be good for the product they are endorsing.

42 A gossip magazine like *heat*, for example, may represent a celebrity in a negative way by printing a photograph of them looking overweight and adding a headline that says something unpleasant about the celebrity.

43 *GQ* is a magazine for men. It is aimed at a slightly older, more sophisticated target audience. Kristen Stewart is represented in quite a sexual way to appeal to a male audience. Her code of gesture is seductive and she is in a luxurious setting, on a sun lounger by the pool. Her clothing of a retro bikini makes her look like an old-fashioned movie star. She is staring directly at the reader. The anchorage of 'Bite Me' is a pun on her role in the *Twilight* films.

44 There are lots of examples to choose from. Think of a star that has something distinctive about them and uses this to market themselves. For example, Olly Murs' 'East end boy' look with his cap and braces.

45 This may include a group of attractive young men 16–20. There will be different personalities and appearances so that fans will have their favourites. Also they will have a backstory of how they met/came together and a catchy hit single to launch them.

46 Social networking sites are ways in which stars can be involved with their fans and can find out their thoughts and opinions about new singles, etc. It is also a way in which they can market themselves to their fans.

47 A star may be more in control of their image when they appear on a chat show and can present themselves in a particular way.

8 Vampire Horror Genre

48 Film posters are important in marketing a film as they are a quick, visual way of showing information about the genre, stars, setting, and release date to an audience.

49 *Brides of Dracula* establishes a villain and a victim. The font style and colour give clues to the genre. The language and characters shown suggest the vampire storyline. The fact that the images are hand-drawn tells us that the poster is older.

50 It is red which suggests blood and danger. The font style is old-fashioned but also looks as if it may have been written in blood, this and the name Dracula tells us that it is a vampire film.

51 Trailers are important as they sum up the narrative briefly and give clues to the film's genre. They use a combination of visual and audio codes to sell the film to an audience but they usually include an enigma to make the audience want to go and see the film.

52 Mainly because audiences are familiar with the Dracula story and this may persuade them to go and see the film. However, they will also expect something a bit different in addition to the original ideas.

53 To appeal to new audiences and because he is the main character. Audiences may like to feel that they know the character, but may also like to be surprised by something different about him.

54 *Twilight* made the vampires appealing to a young audience. They are attractive to look at and we are meant to feel sorry for them because they are unhappy. The romance story between a vampire and a non-vampire was different from anything that had gone before and so it was successful.

9 Music

55 The advantage of targeting a niche audience is that the magazine will have a clear idea of what the fans of the music genre like and are interested in. Once they have built up a loyal audience then they know how to keep them. The disadvantage may be that the niche audience can be small and therefore the magazine will not sell as many copies, so the profits will not be as great as the magazines that target a more mainstream audience.

56 *Vibe* magazine is known for generally featuring R&B and hip hop artists. The front cover features rapper Pharrell and the mysterious duo Daft Punk who belong to these genres. The cover lines feature other artists from these genres.

57 *We Love Pop* is targeted at 13–16 year old girls and so has found a gap in the market, this age group is not really catered for by the music press. It also has regular features and stories linked to artists popular with this age group, One Direction, Little Mix, etc.

58 Both artists are performing. Little Mix are dancing and singing, this is an official, constructed music video so they have direct mode of address with the audience. The Coldplay music video is of a live concert so Chris Martin is seen performing for the live audience, not for the camera.

59 Music videos help to create the star's image because the star is much more in control of what is produced. The narrative, settings and visual codes are all constructed to show a particular view of the star and their music.

60 The 'Parental Advisory' sticker is put in place by the record company to cover themselves in case anyone complains about the content of lyrics. They tell the buyer that the CD may contain explicit phrases and sexual content. However, this may also add to the appeal of the CD! As it suggests, the warning is aimed at parents.

61 Official sites will have higher production values as they belong to the record label and will have more money to produce the site. They will also have good quality images of the band/artist. The unofficial/fan site is much more about the fans themselves. They will include images taken by fans, pictures of fans and messages, blogs, etc., written by fans.

12 Examination Practice and Technique

62 The key terms used to label a magazine cover may include:
- Masthead
- Central image
- Cover lines
- Sell lines
- Splash
- Mode of address.

63 It is important to plan in advance for Section B as you will only have around 40 minutes to complete the whole task and only about 15 minutes for the storyboard/magazine cover task – that is not enough time to think about ideas and get them down on paper.

Glossary

It is very important in all your GCSE examination responses and your internally assessed work that you try to use relevant technical media vocabulary. Doing this will show your understanding and help you to produce a better response. The following list does not include every word you may come across in your study of the media but it does include some useful media terminology to help you to develop your exploration of texts.

ADVERTISING AGENCIES – most makers of products do not make the adverts for the products themselves. They will use an advertising agency whose job it is to research the target audience and then create a campaign to sell the product.

ANCHORAGE – the words that go with the image. They give the image meaning.

ANNOTATE – this means labelling your design to show that you understand the main codes and conventions. This is also your chance to quickly show that you can use the correct media terms.

ASPIRATIONAL – this type of advertising makes the audience want to buy the product even though what it is selling, for example natural beauty and sporting achievement, may be out of their reach.

AUDIO CODES – the different sounds contained within the media text and the connotations attached to the sound used.

AUDIO-VISUAL MEDIA TEXT – one that uses images and/or sound.

BIRD'S EYE VIEW SHOT – this where a scene is shot from overhead. This is often used to film car chases, for example. It allows a lot of the scene to be shown at once but not in any detail.

BRAND – this is how an audience recognise a product and it is also how the product shows it is different from others. The branding may include the name, slogan, logo and any celebrity endorsers.

BRAND IDENTITY – this means the meanings an audience will attach to a particular brand. This will be built up over time. The brand identity of Olay is that it is a reliable and inexpensive product for moisturising skin.

BROADCASTING – this is where a media text tries to attract as wide an audience as possible. For example, the BBC programme *Strictly Come Dancing* includes celebrities from a range of the media to appeal to lots of people.

CAMPAIGN – this is run by an advertising agency, in the case of IRN-BRU, Leith Agency. A campaign is a sequence of advertisements for a product and links the packaging, radio, TV, print and Internet adverts.

CELEBRITY CULTURE – is one where people are obsessed with famous people. These celebrities may not have actually accomplished much, but they often have extensive media coverage.

CHALLENGED – this is where you may investigate a media text that shows a different representation or set of genre conventions to the usual ones. For example, a music video that shows a more realistic example of a young woman or an example of narrative that is not a simple linear structure.

CHRONOLOGICAL – this is a narrative where the events follow in the order in which they happened from beginning to end.

CLEARLY DEFINED ROLES – this means that everyone in the group must have a technical job to do, for example filming, editing or sound. The roles can be shared, for example two people could each do some of the filming and some of the editing, but it must be clear what each person's contribution to the production has been.

CLIFFHANGER – this is where the audience are left with an enigma at the end. This encourages the audience to watch the next episode to find out what happened.

COLLOQUIAL LANGUAGE – this is conversational language where the words used are different from those in written speech.

COMMERCIAL CHANNELS – these are the channels like ITV and Channel 4 that raise their money through advertising, unlike the BBC which currently gets its money from the licence fee.

CONFORM – this means following the rules of a particular genre and including all or most of the main conventions that are shared by similar texts.

CONNOTATIONS – the meanings attached to a sign, for example the use of the colour blue in an advert for toothpaste suggests freshness and cleanliness.

CONSTRUCTION – the way in which the text is put together, for example the choice of font, headline or main image.

CONSUMABLE PRODUCTS – these are products we use regularly and need to replace, for example toothpaste, breakfast cereal, trainers, etc. A successful advert may persuade us to buy something different from the usual.

CONTROLLED ASSESSMENT – is the work that you do in class that then counts towards your final GCSE grade. The assessments are 'controlled' in that you must complete them in class time under your teacher's supervision. They are also controlled by WJEC, the awarding body, as they set the titles from which you must choose.

CONVENTIONAL POINTS OF VIEW – this means that the representation in the text is what is expected by an audience. For example, the representation of the woman in the horror film is as a victim.

CONVENTIONS – what we expect to see in a text belonging to a specific genre.

CONVERGENCE – this is the way in which one topic can be presented across different media forms.

COVER LINES – these usually run down the side and give the reader clues to what is in the magazine. Their aim is to persuade the audience to buy.

CRANE SHOT – this shot is not as extreme as an aerial shot; here the camera is elevated above the action using a crane.

CREDIT SEQUENCE – this is usually the same every week and includes the name of the programme, the stars, the production company, etc. Sometimes this will appear at the start; sometimes it comes after some of the narrative has been introduced.

CULTURAL BACKGROUND – this is what makes you the person you are. It includes where you live, your ethnicity, what you have been brought up to believe in, your religion, etc.

CULTURAL VALUES – this is the idea of what is important or unimportant, right or wrong and is shared by a group of people.

DECODE – the different interpretations of messages by different audiences.

DESENSITISED – this is where an audience is less shocked or upset by violence because they see so much of it in certain media texts.

DIEGETIC SOUND – essentially this is 'sound you can see'; the sound that is part of the scene and can be heard by all the characters, for example the screaming of a character in a horror film.

DIGITALLY ENHANCED – this means that an image is changed on a computer. For example, a computer program can lengthen the neck of the model, get rid of marks on his/her face, make them thinner, straighten their nose, etc.

DIRECT MODE OF ADDRESS – in an audio-visual text, this means that the subject is looking straight at the audience. This involves the audience more.

DISRUPTION – this is what changes the balance in the story world; it may be a character or an event, for example a murder.

DUMBING DOWN – this term refers to the fact that some people think that television programmes are not challenging and that audiences are 'couch potatoes' who just want programmes that are easy to watch.

EDITING – in the production of a film, film-makers will have a lot of footage to choose from. Editing is the way in which the shots and scenes from a film are put together to make a full-length film or a trailer.

EFFECT – the technical code will have been included to have an effect upon the audience. For example, the close-up of a villain's threatening face in a film may make the audience scared.

ENCODE – the ideas and messages that producers package into the texts.

ENDORSE – if celebrities endorse a product they say that they use it and they think it is good. In this way the advertisers hope to persuade the audience, if they like the celebrity, to buy the product.

ENIGMA – this is a mystery or puzzle in the narrative. Enigmas keep an audience interested in the story.

EQUILIBRIUM – this is the state of the story world at the beginning of the narrative where everything is stable.

ETHNICITY – this is something that links you with a particular group of people who share things like customs, food or a way of dressing.

EXPLAIN – where you see this word you will be expected to explore what you have selected in more detail. For example, explaining how and why the camera shots you have chosen have been used.

FLAGSHIP – a programme that is important to the channel as it is popular and audiences recognise it as belonging to the channel, for example *EastEnders* for BBC1.

FORMAL MODE OF ADDRESS – this is used by media texts, for example the news media. The language is complex and the expression serious.

FORMULA – the method for creating something that can be copied, for example a successful boy band.

FRANCHISE – an entire series of the film including the original film and all those that follow on.

GENRE – this is a type of media text that is easily recognisable to audiences.

HIGH KEY LIGHTING – bright lighting usually used to emphasise certain aspects of a scene or image.

HIGH PRODUCTION VALUES – this means that the media text cost a lot to make. You can tell this is the case in an audio-visual text if the locations are exotic and the technical codes are more complex, for example shots from a helicopter.

HOUSE STYLE – this is the 'look' of the magazine that makes it different from other magazines. This may be the font style, the language, mode of address, layout and design or the colours used.

HYBRID GENRE – some programmes share the conventions of more than one genre. *Jonathan Creek* is a crime drama with elements of the paranormal.

HYBRID TEXTS – these are media texts that are difficult to place in one particular genre as they have the elements of different genres. For example, *Dr Who* could be said to be a science fiction/fantasy/drama.

HYPERBOLE – this is over-exaggerated language that makes the text seem very good.

IDENT – this is the way in which the channel can be 'identified'. The ident is a short image that works as a logo for the channel. It usually appears before the programmes. For example, the animated '2' of BBC2.

IDENTIFY – this means 'pick out' or 'find an example of'. For example: Identify two camera shots in this opening sequence.

ILLUSTRATED ESSAY – this is a written piece of work that includes images. For example, if the topic of your investigation is genre conventions in film trailers, you may include some screen shots from your examples to make your point clearer.

INDIRECT MODE OF ADDRESS – where there is no direct contact with the audience. For example, characters in television dramas, unlike in news programmes, do not usually speak directly to the audience.

INFLUENCER – this is where the marketing of a product or service focuses on key people who will 'influence' others into buying the product.

INFORMAL MODE OF ADDRESS – this is where the text adopts a chattier, colloquial style to make the audience feel involved.

INSERT – this is the small booklet that comes inside a CD or DVD. It may contain more images and information.

INTERACTIVE OPPORTUNITIES – this refers to the different ways in which the user of media text can actually become involved.

JINGLE – this is a catchy little song that focuses on the product. Jingles are important for radio adverts as you can't see the product and what it does.

JUSTIFY – this is linked to the examination paper and means explain why you included what you have in your text. For example, why you have used that shot in the storyboard for a television advert. You will also need to say how what you have created will attract an audience.

LANGUAGE – the words used in a media text that may give a clue to its genre. For example, the medical terms used in a programme like *Casualty*.

LINEAR NARRATIVE – this is where the events in the story happen in order, one after another.

LIP SYNCH – this is where the lip movements of the singer are matched up with the vocals. This is usually done at the end when the video is being edited.

LOW KEY LIGHTING – this is where a scene is lit so there is a clear contrast between darkness and shadow. It helps to create a sinister atmosphere.

MAINSTREAM – these are the media texts that are the most popular at the time and also tend to be the most conventional.

MAINSTREAM AUDIENCE – this is a broad target audience. For example, a music magazine would try to include lots of different genres of music and artists in order to appeal to as many people as possible.

MARKETING – this is the way in which the organisation tells its audience about a product. It will use different ways in order to do this, for example a film company will produce trailers and posters to promote a new film. It will also make sure that the stars appear on chat shows and give interviews just before the release of the film.

MASTHEAD – this is the title of the magazine. The name and font style may give a clue to the genre.

MEDIA CONSUMPTION – this is how much of the media we are exposed to and use on a daily basis.

MEDIA HABITS – this refers to the media texts you use regularly, for example watching a soap opera at the same time every week or reading the same magazine each month.

MEDIA ISSUES – these are topics related to the media that are of concern and that are discussed among audiences and in other media texts.

MEDIA ORGANISATIONS – these are the industries and groups that make up the media as a whole, for example television channels, magazine publishers and film companies.

MEDIA PLATFORM – this is a range of different ways of communicating including the Internet, television and newspapers.

MEDIA TEXT – this is something that is produced by a media industry, for example a film.

MERCHANDISE – these are products that you can buy linked to a media text.

MODE OF ADDRESS – this is the way in which a text 'speaks' to its audience. This may be chatty and informal and, as in magazines, for example, may use language only the fans of the genre will understand so making them feel important.

MOOD BOARD – this is a collection of, for example, images, text, and fabrics that help to put together ideas for a production piece.

NARRATIVE – this is the story that is told by the media text.

NARRATIVE STRAND – this is one storyline in the programme/film which may focus on one particular character or event and may run alongside other strands in the same programme/film.

NARROW CASTING – this is where a media text targets a small, very specific audience.

NICHE AUDIENCE – this is a small audience with a specific interest. For example a magazine like *teddy bear times* may be said to have a niche audience.

NON-DIEGETIC SOUND – 'sound you can't see'. This is sound that has been added as part of the post-production process, for example dramatic music in an action film sequence.

NON-LINEAR NARRATIVE – this is where the story moves around in time using techniques like flashbacks.

NON-VERBAL COMMUNICATORS – the way in which signs like facial expressions, clothing and gestures convey messages without the use of words.

OPENING SEQUENCE – this comes after the credit sequence and generally introduces the narrative and the main characters. It may include enigmas to hook the audience and keep them watching.

PAST PAPERS – these are the examination papers that have been set for GCSE Media Studies in previous years. It is useful to see what they look like and the pattern of questions.

PERSONA – the image or personality that someone, for example a celebrity, presents to the audience.

PERSONAL IDENTITY – this means your ability to relate to something that happens in a text because it has happened to you.

PILOT PROGRAMME – this is a one-off programme which is aired to see what the audience response will be. If the response is good then more programmes may be made.

POST-PRODUCTION – this is the term for any production work that takes place on moving or still images after the initial filming or photography shoot has taken place.

PRIME TIME – this is the time when most people watch television and when the most popular programmes are scheduled. It is usually thought to be about 7–9.30pm, although the main family viewing time is 7–8pm.

PRODUCTION VALUES – these are the elements of the text that tell the audience how much it cost to make. A film with high production values will include big name stars, expensive locations or special effects.

PROTAGONIST – this is the main character or characters that move on the action in the crime drama.

PURPOSE – this is the reason why that technical code has been used at that particular time. For example, to increase the tension or to make the audience feel involved in the action.

REACTION SHOT – this is a shot that cuts away from the main scene in the film to show the reaction of a particular character to what has happened. It is commonly used to show an emotional response to something that has happened or has been said.

READING – in Media Studies this refers to your understanding of the text.

RECCE – this refers to a pre-filming visit to possible locations to see if they are suitable for filming. Usually photographs will be taken to record the locations.

REGULATION – these are the rules that control what the media organisation can and can't include in what it produces.

REPRESENTATION – how people, places, issues and events are presented in different media texts in order to create meanings.

REPRESENTATIONS – in production work this means, if you have created a CD cover and insert for a new artist or band, have you considered how to represent them and their style of music through, for example, the use of images, name of the band, font styles, etc.

SCHEDULED – this is the time and day that the programme appears on the television.

SELL LINES – this is the information on the cover that tells the reader what extra they can get if they buy the magazine. They usually 'sell' competitions and free gifts.

SERIAL – a serial has a set amount of episodes. It is made up of one narrative split into episodes with one episode following directly on from another. An audience would have difficulty understanding the middle episode of a serial if they had not watched the previous ones.

SERIES – this is a long-running television programme such as a hospital drama. Each episode of a series has a self-contained storyline and can be watched by a 'one-off' audience. However, it also contains storylines that link one episode to another.

SETTING – the time and place where the action takes place in texts like a film, television programme or music video.

SLOGAN – a short catchy phrase that reminds an audience of the product.

SOCIAL INTERACTION – talking to people about a particular subject.

SPIN-OFF – a new programme that is inspired by an existing one. Links to an existing programme make the new programme easier to market.

STAR IMAGE – the idea that stars want to communicate about themselves to the audience. For example, Lady Gaga uses interviews, public performances and her clothing as well as her music videos to show a specific image that keeps her fans interested.

STEREOTYPES – this is where a group of people are shown in a particular way by exaggerating certain characteristics.

STIMULUS MATERIAL – these are the resources you will be given and asked to respond to in Section A of the examination. They may be audio-visual, for example an extract from a television crime drama, or print, for example two print advertisements, depending on the set topic.

SUB-GENRE – this refers to groups of programmes that share similar conventions, for example a sub-genre of the crime drama genre is detective-led programmes.

SUCCESS CRITERIA – these are the main things you need to include in your work so that you know that you have succeeded.

TAGLINE – this is the short phrase or slogan that appears in trailers and on posters. It gives a clue to the genre and storyline of the film and often includes an enigma.

TARGET AUDIENCE – this is the people at whom the media text is aimed.

TEASER CAMPAIGN – this is where there are several posters for the film. Each one gives a little bit more information running up to the film's release. Teaser posters use enigmas to catch the attention of the audience.

TECHNICAL CODES – the camera shots, angles and movements used to construct the media text.

TEXTUAL INVESTIGATION – this is a piece of work in which you explore one main media text plus examples from others in a topic, for example film posters for science fiction films. This can be presented as a written piece of work like an essay, or as a PowerPoint where you can annotate images. The titles for the Textual investigations are set for you. You must complete this piece of work in school over a set amount of time.

THE MEDIA – a form of mass communication that can give out messages, inform and entertain a large audience.

TOOLKIT – the set of key points that you must refer to when you are exploring a specific media text.

UNIQUE SELLING POINT – unique means different, so this phrase used by advertisers means the product has something about it that is different from other products and this will help to sell it.

USER – this is another word for a type of audience. It suggests that the audience is asked to be active and to 'use' the text in some way. This is usually the case with websites where an audience can watch videos, send in responses and make choices when navigating around the site.

WATER COOLER TELEVISION – this term originated in America and was created to suggest that a programme may be so interesting that people would discuss it around the water cooler at work the next day.

WATERSHED – this is after 9pm and is the time when the channel's suggestion is that the programmes scheduled after this time will not be suitable for younger children. Individual channels have the responsibility for deciding which programmes appear before or after the watershed.

WORD OF MOUTH – this is an unpaid form of advertising where a consumer tells other people how much they like the product. They in turn will tell others. Platforms like Twitter and Facebook have made this quicker and easier.

Index

A

action codes 53
advertising 8, 13, 19, 20, 28, 29, 35, 45, 59–69, 74, 104
  agencies 61, 64
  campaign, analysing 67–69
  techniques 61–63
  types of 60
age 9, 11, 24, 54, 56
anchorage 66, 75–76
apparently impossible positions 53
ASA (Advertising Standards Authority) 68
audience
  age 9, 11, 24, 54, 56
  categorising 59, 64–65
  ethnicity 24, 54
  expectations 30
  gender 24, 54, 56
  involvement 31, 32
  niche 22, 95
  positioning 55
  ratings 26
  research 11
  responding 15, 20, 23–26, 54–56, 58, 74
  target 10, 22, 54, 55, 59, 95–96
  targeting 45–46, 56, 59, 60–61, 68–69
audio codes 18, 22, 33, 50, 54, 58, 63, 88, 90, 91
audio-visual texts, analysing 29–33, 36, 93–94

B

BARB (Broadcasters' Audience Research Board) 45
bird's eye view shot 30, 31, 50
blogs 11, 26
body
  image 12
  language 28
box office numbers 26
brand
  definition of 60
  identity 66
broadcasting 22

C

camera
  angles 17, 29, 30–31, 34, 36, 54
  movement 29, 32
  shots 17, 29–30, 32, 34, 50, 54, 63, 75–76
canted angle shot 31
captions 75
CD covers 102–103
celebrities 12, 13, 62, 66, 73–79
celebrity culture 73, 78
characters 16, 19, 29, 30–32, 41–43, 48–49, 51, 53, 54, 58, 79, 88, 90, 101
chronological 19
circular narrative/structure 19, 51
cliffhanger 52

close-up 28, 30, 34, 100
clothing 17, 21, 28, 34, 54, 66, 76, 86, 102
codes 15, 17–18, 19, 20–21, 22, 27–29, 33, 43, 50, 53, 54, 56, 58, 59, 63, 66, 75–76, 88, 90, 91, 100–101
  audio 18, 22, 33, 50, 54, 58, 63, 88, 90, 91
  technical 17, 20–21, 22, 27, 29–32, 36, 50, 54, 58, 63, 66, 75–76, 88, 91, 101
  visual codes 21, 27, 28–29, 34, 36, 63, 66, 76
colloquial language 35
colour 21, 22, 27, 28, 34, 36, 63, 66, 86, 96–97, 102, 103
commercial channels 45
competition 13, 45, 60, 67
computer games 8, 12
conform 93–94
connotations 27
construction 15, 20, 28–29, 34, 54, 56, 57–58, 67, 75–78, 97, 103
consumable products 60
contextual advertising 64
conventions 15, 16, 41, 43, 48–49, 52, 59, 83, 88–91, 100–104
convergence 93
cover lines 97
crane shot 30, 31
credit sequence 47
crime drama 41–58
cross-media 13
cultural
  backgrounds 24
  diversity 54
  values 78

D

decoding 28
demographic profile 64–65
demonstrative action 63
desensitised 12
design 22, 34, 36, 96–97, 102
dialogue 18, 33, 50
diegetic 33, 63
digitally enhanced 20–21, 29
direct
  mode of address 17, 21, 35, 36, 66, 76, 97, 100, 102
  quotations 35, 36
disruption 51, 67
Dracula 89, 90–91
dumbing down 14
Dyer, Richard 77

E

editing 17, 22, 29, 54, 63, 75, 88, 101
education 24, 56
email marketing 64
encoding 28
endorsement 62, 66, 74

enigmas 19, 46, 52, 53, 85, 86, 88
equilibrium 51, 67
establishing shots 30, 50
ethnicity 24, 54
expression 21, 28, 34, 35, 36, 49, 63, 66, 97, 102
eye level shot 31, 36

F

film posters 20, 21, 29, 85–87
flagship 14, 46
flashback 19, 50, 53, 101
flexi-narrative 52
font style 29, 36, 66, 88, 96, 102
formal mode of address 35
formula 77
franchise 86
front cover 19, 28, 34, 36, 96–98, 102

G

gender 24, 54, 56
genre 10, 15, 16–18, 29, 33, 41–58, 59, 83–92, 95–98, 102, 103
  crime drama 41–58
  horror/vampire 76, 83–92
gesture 28, 34, 102
graphics 29, 47, 88

H

Hammer Horror 91
hard sell 62
headlines 22, 75
high
  angle shot 30
  key lighting 21, 50
horror genre 31, 83–92
house style 96–97
hybrid
  genre 41, 91
  text 16
hyperbole 35, 63, 86

I

iconic representation 63, 66
iconography 16–17, 21, 29, 36, 50, 54, 58, 85, 90–91, 102, 103
ident 15, 46
ideology 78
images 29, 34, 36, 47, 63, 86, 96–97, 102
  central 36, 63, 96–97, 102
imperative 35
indirect mode of address 35
influencer 68
informal mode of address 35
interactive opportunities 104
Internet advertising 64, 68, 104

J

jingle 63

L

language 22, 27, 35, 36, 56, 63, 75, 86, 96–97
layout 22, 34, 36, 96–97, 102
lexis 35, 36
lighting 20, 21, 50, 66, 86
linear narrative/structure 16, 19, 51, 67
lip synch 100
logo 62
long shot 30, 34
low
  angle shot 31, 34, 54
  key lighting 20, 50, 86

M

magazines 8, 19, 22, 25, 35, 45, 60, 74, 76, 78, 95–99
  industry 99
  music 95–99
mainstream 77, 95
marketing 13–14, 43, 59–72, 102
masthead 96–97
media
  consumption 9
  definition of 8
  exposure 10
  forms 37, 83
  habits 9–11
  issues 11–12
  organisations 13–14, 15, 44–46, 59
  texts 8–9, 15, 16, 25–36, 53–55, 74, 75–76, 78, 84–92, 95–98
medium shot 30
merchandise 95, 104
mode of address 17, 21, 22, 35, 36, 56, 63, 66, 75–76, 96–97, 100, 102
mood board 110
movement 17
music 8, 18, 22, 33, 46, 47, 50, 54, 63, 77, 88–89, 95–104
  videos 8, 100–101

N

narrative 15, 16, 19, 41, 46, 50, 51–53, 58, 59, 67, 86, 88, 101
  GCSE audio visual textual investigation 57–58
  music video 101
  strands 52
narrow casting 22
negotiated reading 25
newspapers 8, 45, 60
niche audience 22, 95
non-diegetic 33, 63
non-linear narrative/structure 19, 51
non-verbal communicators 28
Nosferatu 83, 90

O

objects 16–17, 86, 102
opening sequence 47, 92
oppositional reading 25
organisations 13–14, 15, 44–46, 59, 89–92
originality 62

P

pan 32
persona 77–78
personal identity 24, 25, 57
pilot programme 45
plot 16
point of view shot 31, 53
pop under 64
pop up 64
post-production 34
preferred reading 25
presentation 14, 57, 93
prime time 44
print
    advertisements, analysing 66
    texts, analysing 33–35, 36, 71–72
privileged spectator position 53
production
    assignment/piece 40, 70, 92–93, 99
    values 86, 100
promotion 13–14, 85, 100; *also see* marketing
protagonists 48
psychometric profiling 65

Q

quality mark 86
quotes 35, 36, 86

R

radio 8, 13, 45
ratings 26, 45
reaction shot 32
reading media text 25–26
recce 110
regulation 13–14, 15, 68
representation 15, 20–21, 53–55, 59, 63, 66, 67, 75–76,
    90–92, 102–103
research 11, 13, 14, 18, 80, 99, 106–110
reviews 26

S

scheduling 10, 44, 45
script 18
search engine marketing 64
sell lines 96–97
serial, definition of 48
series, definition of 46
setting 16–17, 41, 50, 58, 86, 90
sign, definition of 27
slang 35
slogan 60, 61
social
    interaction 24, 25, 56
    networking 12, 56, 68, 73, 78, 104
soft sell 63
sound effects 18, 33, 63, 88–89
special effects 17, 91
spin-off 43

split screen narratives 52
star
    image 100
    theory 77
stars 16, 43, 45, 46, 77–79, 85, 86, 100
stereotypes 20–21, 54, 59, 101
stimulus material 38–39
Stoker, Bram 83
storyboard 93, 111
stripping 44
sub-genre 41–43, 48

T

tagline 85, 86, 88
target audience 10, 22, 54, 55, 59, 95–96
technical codes 17, 20–21, 22, 27, 29–32, 36, 50, 54, 58, 63,
    66, 75–76, 88, 91, 101
    effect 30
    purpose 30
technique 29, 34
television crime drama 41–58
tension 18, 30, 33, 52, 53
Textual investigation 40, 71–72, 81–82, 89, 105, 120–121
three screen narratives 52
tilt 32
Todorov 19, 51
toolkit for analysis 27–36
tracking shot 32
trailers 46, 88–89
Twilight 76, 86, 88, 91
Twitter 68, 73, 78, 104
two-parter 44

U

unique selling point (USP) 62, 77
user, definition of 69
uses and gratifications theory 24, 56–57

V

vampire genre 76, 83–92
visual codes 21, 27, 28–29, 34, 36, 63, 66, 76
voice-overs 33, 46, 53, 88–89

W

'water-cooler' television 56
watershed 13, 44
web banners 64
websites 8, 26, 64, 69, 103–104
word of mouth marketing 68

Y

Young and Rubicam 65

Z

zoning 44
zoom 32

Image credits

The publishers wish to acknowledge and thank the following for images used in this book:

p14 Ofcom logo © Ofcom, Office of Communications;
p14 bbfc logo © bbfc, British Board of Film Classification;
p14 ASA logo © ASA, Advertising Standards Authority;
p15 *Born Risky* logo © Channel 4;
p16 *I'm a Celebrity, Get Me out of Here* (2013) ITV Studios;
p16 *Holby City* (2013), BBC;
p17 *Iron Man 3* (2013) Marvel/Paramount/Shane Black;
p18 *Casualty* (2013) BBC;
p18 Script from *Casualty* (2007) Series 22, Episode 11, Daisy Coulan/BBC;
p19 *Match of the Day* (2012) BBC;
p20 Rex Features (2011);
p20 L'Oreal/McCann Erickson;
p21 *Kidulthood* (2006) TMC/Cipher/Stealth/ Menhaj Huda;
p21 Maybelline/McCann (2011);
p22 *Dogs Today*;
p22 elliegoulding.com/Polydor;
p23, 35 *PlayStation* (2013) Future Publishing Ltd;
p23 *The Hunger Games: Catching Fire* (2013) Lionsgate/Francis Lawrence;
p25 *Men's Fitness* (2014) Dennis Publishing Ltd;
p28 *Black Veil Brides: Set the World on Fire* (2011) Lava Records/Universal Republic Records;
p29 *Ender's Game* (2013) Odd Lot Entertainment/Gavin Hood;
p31 *Gladiator* (2000) Dreamworks/Universal/Scott Ridley;
p31 *Silence of the Lambs* (1991) Orion/Jonathan Demme;
p34 *Total Film* (2013) Future Publishing Ltd;
p36, 97 *Kerrang!* (2013) Bauer Media;
p42, 47, 55 *Scott & Bailey* (2013) Red Production Company/Sarah Pia Anderson;
p42 *CSI: Miami* (2012) CBS Television Studios/Jerry Bruckheimer;
p43 *Inspector Morse, Lewis, Endeavour* (1987–2014) Zenith/Central Independent Television/ITV Studios;
p44 *Broadchurch* review (2013) TV Times/IPC+ Syndication;
p45 Immediate Media/*Radio Times* (2012) ;
p46 *BBC One Ident* (2007) BBC;
p47, 50, 55 *Luther* (2011, 2013) BBC Drama;
p48 *Lewis* (2006 –) ITV Studios;
p48 *Silent Witness* (1996–) BBC;
p49 *Ripper Street* (2012–) Tiger Aspect/BBC/Tom Shankland;
p49 *Case Histories* (2011–2013) Ruby/BBC/Marc Jobst, Dan Zeff;
p49, 52, 54 *CSI* Series 12 (2011–12) CBS;
p49 *Murder She Wrote* (1984–1996) Universal/CBS;
p49 *Broadchurch* (2013)/Kudos/ITV/James Strong;
p49 *New Tricks* (2013) BBC/Philip John;
p52 *The Killing (Forbrydelsen)* (2007–2012) Danmarks Radio;
p55, 58 *Vera* (2011–2014) ITV Productions;

p56 *Sherlock* (2010–) BBC Wales;
p62 *Swoosh* Nike Inc;
p62 *Unloved Rooms* (2013) B&Q/Lalli Johnson/Kream/Karmarama;
p62 *Dance Pony Dance* (2013) 3/Dougal Wilson/Blink/Wieden + Kennedy;
p63 *Trésor* (1996) Peter Lindbergh/Lancôme/L'Oreal;
p64 Jet2Holidays.com;
p66 Olay (2012) Hill & Knowlton/Procter and Gamble;
p67–69 IRN-BRU/Leith Agency/AG Barr;
p74 *Elvive*/McCann Erickson/L'Oreal;
p75 *Daily Express* (2012);
p75 *The Sun* (2012);
p76 Norman Jean Roy/*GQ* © The Condé Nast Publications Ltd;
p78 *heat (2013)* Bauer Media;
p79 *Snow White and The Huntsman* (2012) Universal/Rupert Sanders;
p79 Mario Testino/*Vogue* © The Condé Nast Publications Ltd.
p79 *Us Weekly* LLC (2012);
p84, 90 *Dracula* (1931) Universal/Tod Browning;
p84, 90 *Nosferatu, eine Symphonie des Grauens* (1922) Prana Film/FW Murnau;
p84, 85, 87 *Dracula* (1958) Hammer Film Productions/Terence Fisher;
p84, 86, 87, 91 *Twilight* (2008) Summit Entertainment/Catherine Hardwicke;
p84 *Die Gruft von Graf Dracula* (1974) Williams Verlag;
p84, 87 *Låt den Rätte Komma In (Let the Right One In)* (2008) Fido Film/Thomas Alfredson;
p84 *30 Days of Night* (2007) Ghost House/Columbia/Dark Horse/David Slade;
p86 *Interview with a Vampire* (1994) Geffen Pictures/Neil Jordan;
p86, 89 *Byzantium* (2012) Demarest Films/Neil Jordan;
p86 *Twilight: New Moon* (2009) Summit Entertainment/Chris Weitz;
p87, 88, 91 *Bram Stoker's Dracula* (1992) Zoetrope/Columbia Tri-Star/Francis Ford Coppola;
p87 *The Lost Boys* (1987) Warner Bros/Joel Schumacher;
p96 *Vibe* (2013) Spin Media;
p96, 98 *We Love Pop* Magazine © Egmont UK Ltd. Logo © Universal Music Operations Ltd;
p100 *Christmas Lights* (2010), Coldplay, Capitol/Parlophone /Mat Whitecross;
p100 *Move* (2013), Little Mix, Nathan Duvall, Maegan Cottone, Sycho/Columbia;
p101 *I Know You Care* (2012), Ellie Goulding, Justin Parker/Polydor;
p101 *Dear Darlin'* (2013), Olly Murs, Ed Drewett, Jim Eliot Epic/Sycho/Columbia;
p103 *Prism* (2013) Katy Perry, Capitol;
p103 *Get Rich or Die Tryin'* (2003), 50 Cent, Aftermath/Universal;
p104 onedirectionmusic.com, Sycho/Sony;

The following Shutterstock.com contributors: p6: Tomislav Pinter; p8: Stuart Miles; p9: Adam Ziaja; p10: David Grigg; p11: jwblinn; p13: Pavel L Photo and Video; p15: login; p23: Petr Jilek; p24: Michael C. Gray ; p27: issumbosi, Laschon Maximilian; p29: Rido; p30: FuzzBones, Hipgnosis, Tatiana Kostenko; p33: Maxim Tarasyugin, Pavel K, wavebreakmedia; p37: Tatiana Kostenko, wavebreakmedia; p39: everything possible; p40: FuzzBones; p41: Fer Gregory; p53: Dutourdumonde Photography; p59: My Life Graphic; p65: Melica, Ysbrand Cosijn, Zvonimir Atletic; p70: Grounder; p73: Featureflash;, JStone, s_bukley; p77: Photo Works, Jaguar PS; p78: Featureflash; p84: Memo Angeles; p92: Nikiteev_Konstantin; p95: Amir Ridhwan; p103: zeber; p112: Chris Rawlins, Tsian; p113: Designer things, zeber; p118: DAIVI, ideldesign ; p121: wavebreakmedia; p122: Filipe Matos Frazao; p127: damato; p128: life_in_a_pixel; p130: Ivelin Radkov, majabokun

Fotolia: p60: ©vege

Cover photograph: © Miguel A. Muñoz Pellicer/Alamy